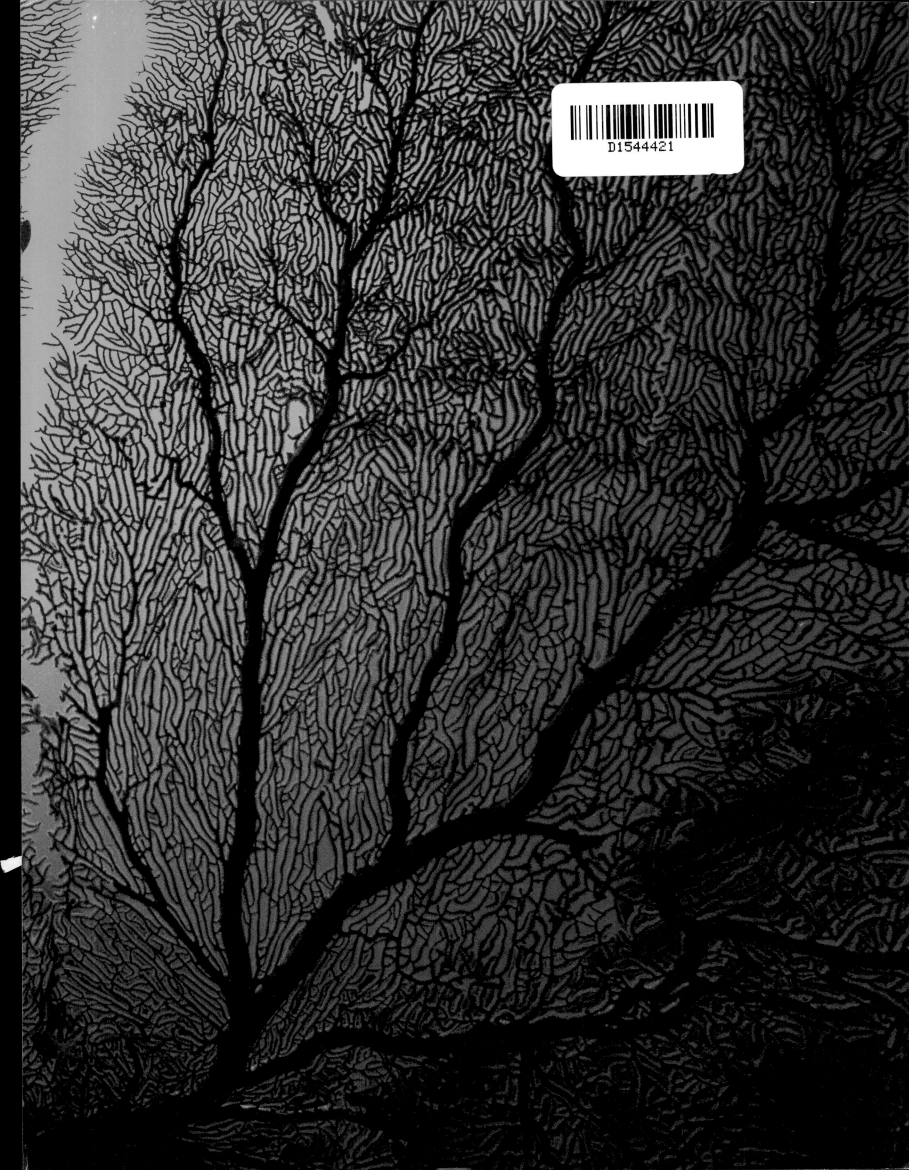

To my friend, dive-buddy, & "cuz": memories of ALDABRA & your 66th

THANKS FOR SAVING MY WIFE FROM THE SHARK...

Kevin + Kristine

To increasing quality as well as quantity in this 67th year and beyond.

It is an honor to be with you and your wonderful wife on your 66th birthday — I still think someone seriously miscounted that! You and Jid are a true inspiration.

Steve Brown

To John... A long life of love and Comfort

Det är lika trevligt varje gång att få träffa Dig och Jid. En gladare och mer positiv människa möter man sällan.

ALDABRA

ALDABRA

WORLD HERITAGE SITE

SEYCHELLES ISLANDS FOUNDATION

MOHAMED AMIN • DUNCAN WILLETTS • ADRIAN SKERRETT

FOREWORD BY SIR DAVID ATTENBOROUGH

ACKNOWLEDGEMENTS

Thanks are due to David Stoddart, who first proposed the concept for this book in 1986; and to Maryse Eichler, who was first charged with the task of formulating ideas. Without the full support of Maurice Loustau-Lalanne, Chairman of the Seychelles Islands Foundation, this book could never have been completed.

The staff of the Seychelles National Archives were, as always, extremely helpful and efficient, and thanks are due to them all, in particular Madame Sinon. Access to this collection was fascinating and essential.

To reach Aldabra, the crew of the catamaran *Stephanie* — Bennie, Dan, and Arab — provided excellent facilities, good humour, and good food. The Seychelles Underwater Centre provided support to the underwater photographers and donated their equipment for the divers. The land-based team was given superb support by Aldabra Manager Pat Bijoux, who bent over backwards to ensure the whole atoll was covered by the team. 'Rock' Lozaique (alias 'Ti Frans') offered knowledge of the tides and sea conditions, supported by Jean 'Marmay' Nicholas, while Bernard Legae (alias 'Ton Ben') acted as guide and Angela Eliza as cook. Goat hunters Ray Rainbolt and Bruce Schoeberl assisted with guiding, including tracking down the elusive flamingo. Ian Stirling, Chris Huxley and David Rowat assisted in checking the drafts of some chapters. Judith Skerrett researched literature to provide quotes to head each chapter, typed the manuscript, and acted as Assistant Editor.

Last, but not least, thanks are due to all the contributors who gave their time, energy, and knowledge freely to the Seychelles Islands Foundation in order to produce this book.

Endpapers: Gorgonian fan coral; a filigree of lace silhouetted on the blue ocean depths. Half title: Adult male lesser frigatebird inflates its scarlet throat patch in an attempt to attract a mate. Title page: Mushroom islets in the huge lagoon are havens for nesting seabirds.

CONTENTS

*Pages 10-11: Schools of exuberant spinner dolphins
are a common sight in the deep waters close to the reef edge of
Aldabra; Pages 12-13: Aldabra the green: a narrow girdle of land
encircles the shallow waters of the vast lagoon. This is the
world's largest raised coral atoll; Pages 14-15: Aldabra's nearest
neighbour and airlink with the outside world is the raised coral
platform island of Assumption. Exploited and laid waste, a
poignant reminder of the fate which Aldabra mercifully escaped;
Pages 16-17: Cosmoledo, the second largest atoll of the Aldabra Group.*

FOREWORD

Aldabra is one of the wonders of the world. It is so because the rest of the world is so far away from it. This isolation has given it animals and plants that make it unique. It has the largest population of giant tortoises anywhere in the world. They are of a different kind and very much more numerous than the celebrated ones that live on the Galapagos Islands. It is the home of the only remaining flightless bird in the Indian Ocean. It provides nesting grounds for great numbers of spectacular ocean-going birds such as frigates and boobies. It even has plants and birds that are identifiably different from any to be found elsewhere.

Other islands in the Indian Ocean once had similar marvels. There were giant tortoises in Madagascar and on the Comoro Islands. They are now gone. There were flightless birds on Mauritius and Réunion. They have gone too. All were destroyed unthinkingly and carelessly by human beings.

The isolation that brought Aldabra's unique animals into existence is so extreme that so far, it has also saved them. The island is so distant from all other land and so far from normal shipping routes that, although men for millennia sailed throughout the Indian Ocean, very few reached Aldabra until recently. But now time is catching up. In the 1960s, there was a proposal to turn the island into a military base and build an airstrip for bombers over its lagoon. Conservationists worldwide united to protest against such an outrage. Happily this was one of the battles that conservation won.

Today Aldabra's isolation has been reduced still further. It is now easier to reach the island than it has ever been in history. From now on, the dangers threatening it can only increase. If it is to survive undamaged, humanity at large will have to be convinced that Aldabra is one of the world's greatest surviving natural treasures. That is the aim of this book. I believe it succeeds brilliantly and it is a privilege to commend it.

David Attenborough

*Opposite: At anchor in the sunset, one of the few charter yachts
that visit Aldabra each year is silhouetted against a fiery sky.*

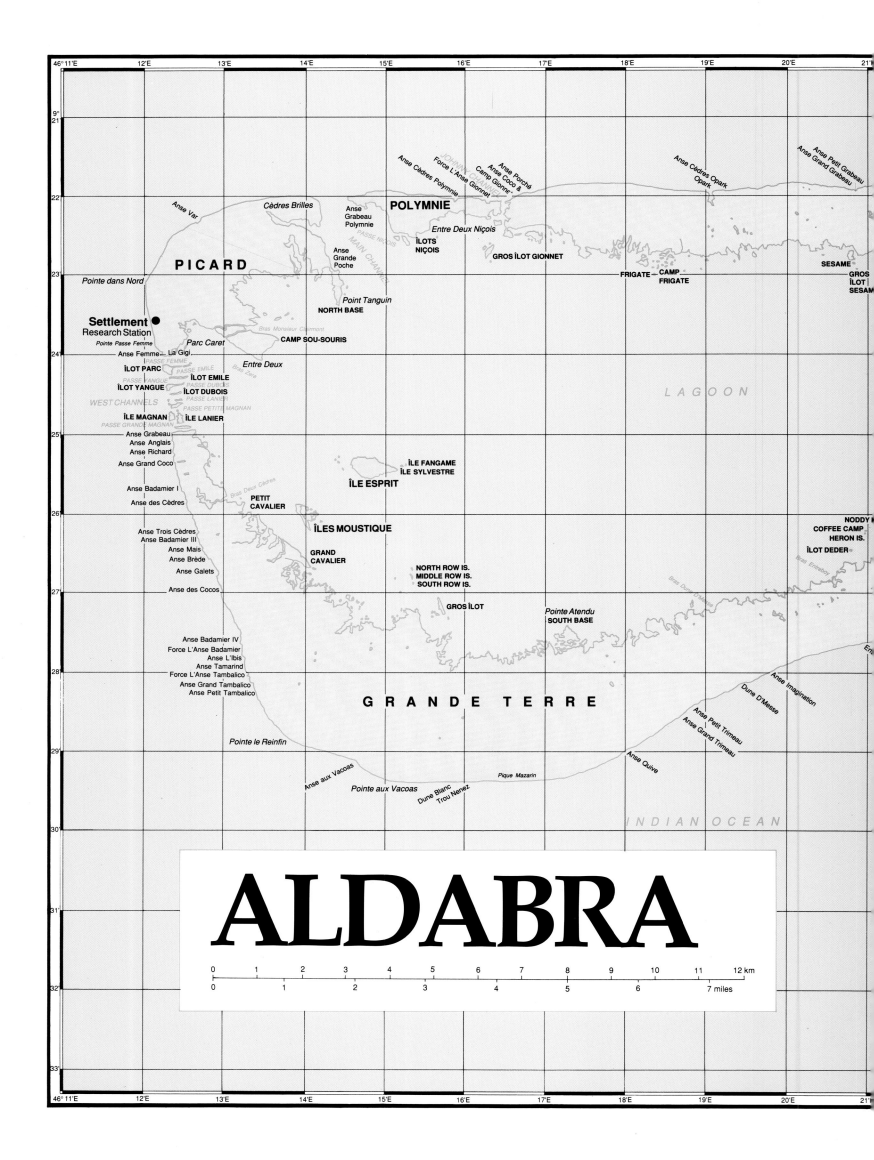

ALDABRA

0	1	2	3	4	5	6	7	8	9	10	11	12 km

0	1	2	3	4	5	6	7 miles

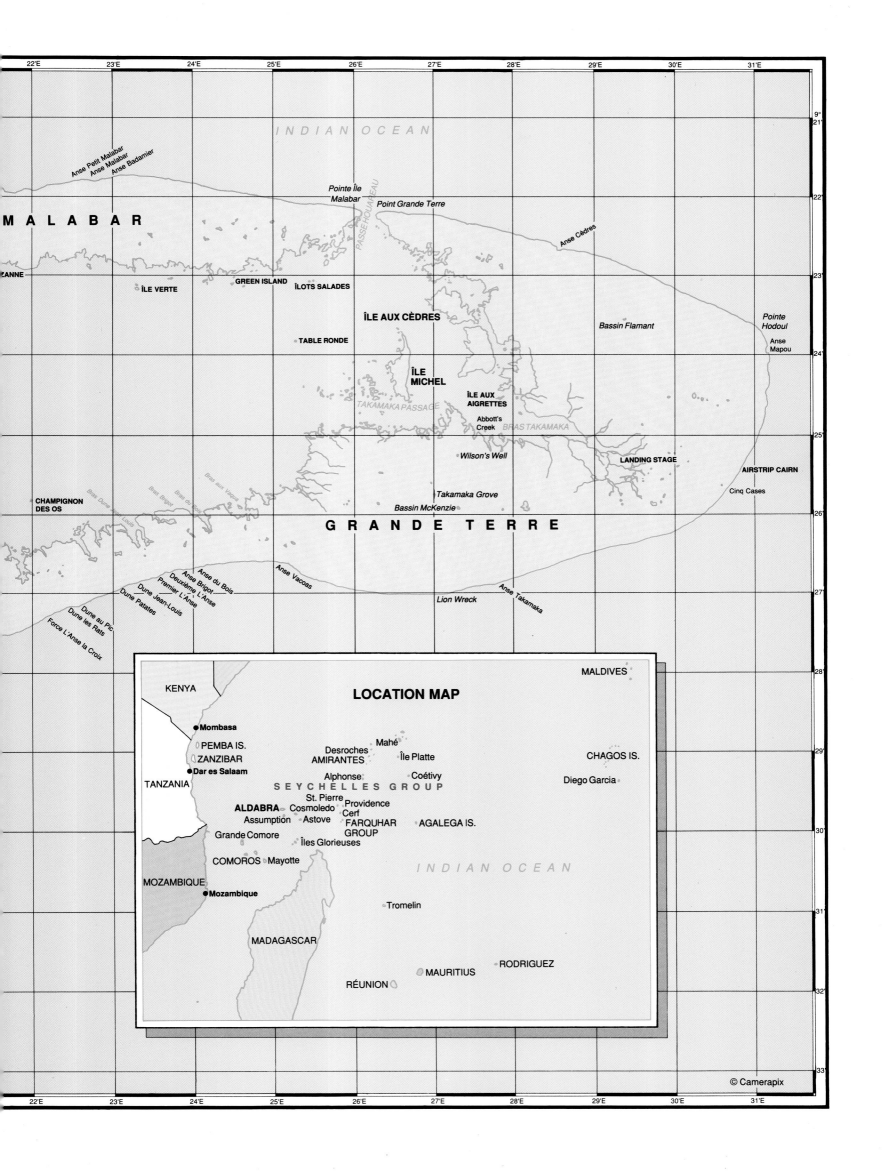

INDIAN OCEAN

Anse Petit Malabar
Anse Malabar
Anse Badamier

MALABAR

Pointe Île
Malabar
Point Grande Terre

Anse Cèdres

ANNE

ÎLE VERTE

GREEN ISLAND

ÎLOTS SALADES

ÎLE AUX CÈDRES

Bassin Flamant

Pointe
Hodoul

TABLE RONDE

ÎLE
MICHEL

Anse
Mapou

TAKAMAKA PASSAGE

ÎLE AUX
AIGRETTES

Abbott's
Creek

BRAS TAKAMAKA

Wilson's Well

LANDING STAGE

AIRSTRIP CAIRN

CHAMPIGNON
DES OS

Bras Dune Jean Louis

Bras Brigot

Bras du Bois

Bras aux Vagues

Takamaka Grove

Bassin McKenzie

Cinq Cases

GRANDE TERRE

Anse du Bois
Anse Brigot
Deuxième L'Anse
Premier L'Anse
Dune Jean-Louis
Dune Patates
Dune au Pic
Dune les Rats
Force L'Anse la Croix

Anse Vacoas

Lion Wreck

Anse Takamaka

MALDIVES

KENYA

LOCATION MAP

Mombasa

PEMBA IS.

ZANZIBAR

Desroches

Mahé

Île Platte

CHAGOS IS.

AMIRANTES

Dar es Salaam

Alphonse

Coétivy

Diego Garcia

TANZANIA

SEYCHELLES GROUP

St. Pierre

Providence

ALDABRA

Cosmoledo

Cerf

FARQUHAR
GROUP

AGALEGA IS.

Assumption

Astove

Grande Comore

Îles Glorieuses

COMOROS

Mayotte

INDIAN OCEAN

MOZAMBIQUE

Mozambique

Tromelin

MADAGASCAR

RODRIGUEZ

MAURITIUS

RÉUNION

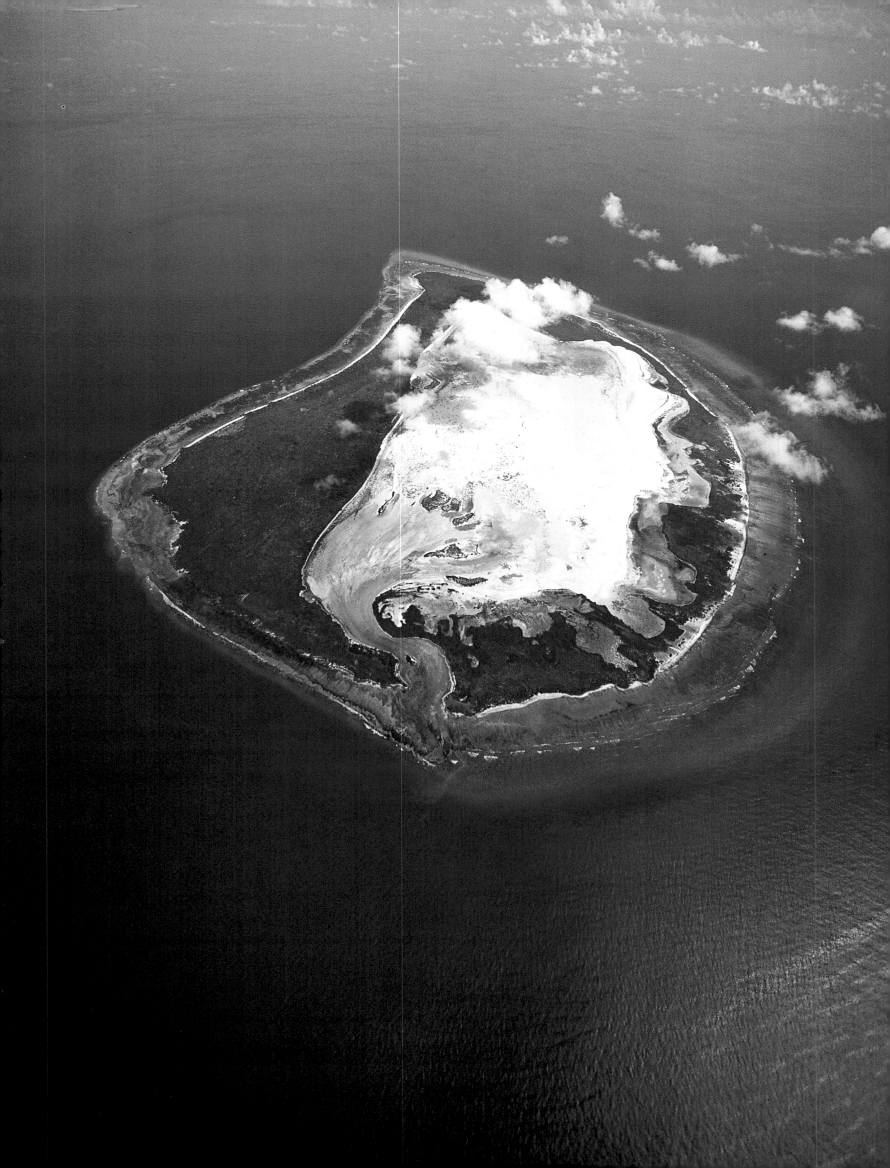

INTRODUCTION
A VIRGIN LAND
GUY LIONNET

'Behind every site on the World Heritage List there is undoubtedly a story to be told. But the story of Aldabra is exceptional by virtue of containing all the elements of a dramatic novel: hidden treasure on a faraway tropical island; a scheme to annex the island for military purposes; a counter-campaign to save the island and its unspoilt wildlife; secret agreements; a last-minute reprieve from unexpected quarters; international recognition and protection of the island and its treasure; and, finally, a grand gesture by the government of the Seychelles.'
ALDABRA ATOLL: A STUNNING SUCCESS STORY
D.R. Stoddart & J.D.M. Ferrari

*Above: The giant tortoise is King of Aldabra, but even for them,
negotiation of the terrain is far from easy.
Opposite: The tiny jewel of Astove, one of the Aldabra Group, lying in the extreme south-
western corner of Seychelles has
claimed many shipwrecks on its encircling reefs.*

A

LDABRA, ASSUMPTION, COSMOLEDO AND Astove constitute the Aldabra group of islands in the Republic of Seychelles. Lying north-west of Madagascar, they are the extreme south-western limit of Seychelles, whose 115 islands are spread between Madagascar and the equator. The Aldabra group is unusual in that the islands are raised coral atolls and platform reefs. Indeed, Aldabra is the world's largest raised atoll.

Aldabra may owe its name to the Arabic *al-khadra,* meaning 'the green', which is also the Arab name for the island of Pemba off the East African coast. However, the origin of this name could also be ascribed to the fact that Aldabra's huge lagoon produces a green reflection in the sky, which can be perceived at a large distance at sea. A further suggestion is that the name was taken from another Arabic word, *al-dabaran,* which refers to five stars in the Taurus group, in particular the brightest of these by which the Arabs navigated, and perhaps located the atoll.

Undoubtedly known to early Arab navigators, Aldabra was mentioned on Portuguese charts and later by the French who sailed from Mauritius during the eighteenth century to reconnoitre a direct route between that island and India. As a dependency of Mauritius, Aldabra was to become British by the 1814 Treaty of Paris and to be joined to Seychelles in 1881. However, in 1965 Aldabra was detached from Seychelles to form part of the newly created British Indian Ocean Territory, but was returned to Seychelles in 1976 upon independence.

Due to its isolation, away from the main shipping routes, and its lack of exploitable natural resources, Aldabra was to escape the fate of Assumption, its closest neighbour, which was quarried for guano and thus laid waste. Later, Aldabra was to receive special recognition for its extraordinary ecosystem. First declared a nature reserve of Seychelles, Aldabra then became a UNESCO World Heritage Site in 1982. It is managed, together with the Vallée de Mai on Praslin (the second World Heritage Site of Seychelles), by Seychelles Islands Foundation, a non-government organization whose board of trustees includes the well-known scientific institutions the Royal Society of London, the Smithsonian Institute of Washington, ORSTOM of Paris, the Royal Society for Nature Conservation of the UK and the International Union for Conservation of Nature and Natural Resources.

On Picard (one of the islands making up Aldabra's atoll ring) there is a research station established and built by the Royal Society in 1971, when Aldabra formed part of the British Indian Ocean Territory. It is managed today by Seychelles Islands Foundation, but is open to researchers from all over the world. What is so extraordinary about Aldabra and its ecosystem? The answer is its geology, its flora and, of course, its fauna.

Aldabra atoll is situated on a submarine volcanic pinnacle. Its history is told by fossils of giant tortoises, crocodiles and iguanas found within its coral foundation. Over the long course of geological time it has undergone several submersions and emergences due to sea level variations. Today Aldabra consists of a large central lagoon and a split ring of small islands whose fossil corals recall a lunar landscape. The atoll is some thirty-five kilometres

long and fourteen kilometres wide, with a total land area of about 140 square kilometres. The atoll rim surrounds a huge lagoon which is connected to the sea by several deep channels through which the tides flow, providing fresh influxes of water twice daily. These channels (Main Channel, Johnny Channel or Passe Gionnet, West Channels and Passe Houareau) divide the atoll ring into four main islands: Grande Terre (South Island), Picard, Polymnie, and Malabar. Also, there are many small islands and islets in the lagoon, of which the two largest are named Esprit and Michel.

The outside of the atoll, facing the ocean, consists mainly of very low coral limestone cliffs and white coral sand beaches. Inside the lagoon, there are also mangrove swamps and, at low tide, vast expanses of sand and mud.

It was probably some 125,000 years ago, after its last emergence, that the first members of its present flora and fauna began to reach Aldabra, mainly from Madagascar, and started to evolve on the atoll.

Among the nearly 200 plant species found on Aldabra, some twenty-two per cent are endemic (that is, found nowhere else on earth). The plants are found among the mangroves, on the elevated dunes, and in the almost impenetrable pemphis thickets. There are arid terrains, small woodland groves in depressions where some soil has accumulated, and grassy stretches that are the pastures where giant tortoises graze. Striking plants of Aldabra include the Aldabra lily (*Lomatophyllum aldabraense*), whose large orange-red flowers stand out clearly on the grey coral landscape, the jasmine (*Jasminum elegans*), the *bwa bouke* (*Ochna ciliata*) which, when in bloom, is covered with bright yellow flowers, and at least two interesting orchid species.

Aldabra's butterflies are the most beautiful of Seychelles. Mainly of Malagasy origin, they include two colourful nymphalids of the genus *Junonia*, one of which, *Junonia rhadama*, is a real gem with its metallic blue colour, and several acraeids, especially the subspecies *Acraea terpsicor legrandi*, whose transparent forewings have a delicate red tint.

The star animal of Aldabra is the giant tortoise, still found there in very great numbers. This antediluvian reptile has disappeared from the rest of the world, except on the Galapagos Islands in the Pacific Ocean. There are some 150,000 giant tortoises on Aldabra, while on the Galapagos Islands, reputed the world over for their tortoises, there are only about 10,000. Only on Aldabra is a large herbivorous reptile the dominant animal. Because of this it is of utmost importance to preserve the atoll. A fascinating discovery in the Cerin Jurassic quarries in France of fossilized tracks of giant tortoises reminds us of the similarity between today's Aldabra and palaeo-ecosystems of yesterday. This is another captivating aspect of Aldabra, that it is, as Pearson Phillips put it, 'a place reminiscent of those stories in schoolboy annuals about miraculous territories beyond inaccessible mountain ranges peopled by dinosaurs.'

The Aldabran birds include a great variety of seabirds and unique land birds, of which the white-throated rail is the only remaining flightless bird of the region.

Aldabra is the last stronghold of the green turtle in Seychelles. Exploited almost to extinction in the granite islands, and decimated elsewhere, including the neighbouring island of Assumption, the Aldabran population is an important reservoir for this species if it is to be saved for future generations.

The pristine reefs of Aldabra offer spectacular underwater opportunities to those lucky enough to visit the atoll. Life on Aldabra revolves around the tides to a great extent. The water surges through the narrow channels with tremendous force, breathing new life into the lagoon twice a day, and bringing with it a host of fish and other sea creatures.

Virtually unspoilt by man, Aldabra is a virgin land where plants and animals exist in a natural but fragile equilibrium. This could easily be upset by man and his machines. To preserve and protect it, so that our children's children may enjoy it, Aldabra should be left to itself. It should be a sanctuary untouched and untouchable. It deserves no less.

1

SOMEWHERE IN AN EMPTY OCEAN

JUDITH SKERRETT AND LEN MOLE

'Some called it the island man forgot; from all accounts it was a pity it had ever been remembered.'
ALDABRA ALONE
Tony Beamish

Above: As though flying underwater, a hawksbill turtle skims
gracefully over the reef.

IT COULD BE SAID THAT ALDABRA HAS no history prior to the late nineteenth century in that there is next to no *human* history. Of course, massive geological and biological events were shaping the Aldabra we know today, and we cannot discount the idea that the atoll had human visitors before those who arrived in the eighteenth century. In 1511, Aldabra, named as Alhadra, appears on a Portuguese map of Madagascar. This may imply that the Portuguese landed there, but the character of the name given to the island also almost certainly suggests that Aldabra was known first to the Arabs. The Arabs are reported to have reached Madagascar as early as 916AD, and in the fourteenth century they were journeying up the East African coast and across to the Maldives. They had been settled in East Africa since the seventh century, and undertook voyages of discovery and trade into the Indian Ocean, arriving in Mauritius, Reunion, and Rodriguez as well as the Comoros. Given their criss-crossing of this region of ocean, it seems almost inevitable that they should have stumbled upon Aldabra.

The Portuguese leaned heavily on Arab knowledge of the area during their own fifteenth- and sixteenth-century navigations in the Indian Ocean, copying their charts and employing Arab pilots on their ships. For example, Vasco da Gama was advised by an Arab pilot during his 1498 voyage from Malindi in East Africa to Calicut in India.

All that we have from this time on are a series of distorted names on the charts, until 1742, when a short description and map appear in the log of the French Captain Lazare Picault, who thought he was at Jean de Nova (then the name of Farquhar). He sighted the atoll on Monday 29th October and anchored just before midday. The following day a party went ashore, taking careful note of the large numbers of giant tortoises, 'of which the smallest was bigger than the biggest on Rodriguez island; there are some there that six men could not carry.' They also were rapidly discovered to be 'much more tender and better tasting' than those of Rodriguez.

Picault was surprised that, despite the large size of the island he found himself on (which seems to have been Picard — perhaps explaining the origin of that name), they could find no fresh water. He sent men to the interior in search of it, but they returned unsuccessful and 'pressed with thirst'. Since they were short of water, and the anchorage was insecure due to strong currents, they loaded as many tortoises as they could carry and sailed on the morning of 1st November 1742. Much as he had enjoyed the tortoise meat, Picault decided that 'the place is not good for anything except to refresh oneself'. He sailed on to fulfil his mission of exploring the granitic Seychelles. Aldabra, and its tender, tasty tortoises, were left in peace again.

From that November day, Aldabra slips back into oblivion. The central granitic islands of Seychelles, and their coralline satellites, were one by one possessed by the French as from 1756. The most accessible islands were settled from 1770 onwards. Aldabra, remote and considered 'not good for anything', became a sort of 'no man's land'. There was no one there to worry about defending sovereignty anyway.

Time may have stood still on Aldabra, but elsewhere the world was changing. In the

course of the Napoleonic Wars, the French lost Mauritius to the British in 1811. In that year, Mahé was also formally taken by the British and in subsequent renewals of the Treaty of Paris (1814 and 1815) Aldabra, like Seychelles, became a British dependency governed from Mauritius, the mother colony.

The British were at first unsure as to the contents of their new Indian Ocean 'package'; a bewildering array of islands, atolls, sand banks, and cays scattered all over the region north and west of Mauritius. Aldabra was a 'grey area' for the administrators, who were probably relieved that there seemed to be so little there worth worrying about. No one took much notice of the parties of fishermen from the granitic islands who took up temporary abode there while stocking up with fish, turtle and tortoises. Jean-Francois Hodoul, a successful privateer during the war, then settled in central Seychelles, is supposed to have organized one such 'fishing camp' on Aldabra, and there is a Point Hodoul (the most easterly point) there today. Whatever it may have said on the legal documents in London, Aldabra was still regarded by everyone else as 'open house', since the British showed no sign of making any settlement there.

Then, in 1874, the authorities on Mauritius decided to take some action on Aldabra. They planned a wood-cutting enterprise. Aldabra has extensive stands of mangrove; mangrove

bark yields a red die, making it a valuable commodity at the time, and the straight mangrove poles were also useful for construction.

News of this proposed exploitation reached London, where certain persons, most notably Charles Darwin and Dr Gunther at the British Museum of Natural History, were already concerned about the population of giant tortoises on Aldabra, since the species was now extinct throughout the rest of the region. Darwin and others appealed to the Governor of Mauritius to take steps to preserve the tortoises, expressing concern that these 'Gigantic Land Tortoises…the last remains of this animal form…known to exist in a state of nature' would now also be threatened with extinction. 'The rescue and protection of these animals,' the letter continues, 'is recommended less on account of their utility…than on account of the great scientific interest attached to them.'

From this moment on, the British administrators did make efforts, albeit somewhat half-heartedly, to protect the giant tortoises of Aldabra, although all other natural resources of the atoll, such as the turtles, were still regarded as 'fair game'. The proposed wood-cutting project was dropped.

Aldabra's next official visitors were the men of *HMS Fawn*, a survey ship. Because of the concern in London as to the fate of the giant tortoises, Dr Gunther asked that specimens should be collected for the museum by Captain Wharton of *HMS Fawn* during the visit. Dr Gunther had only been able to obtain full-grown specimens before by paying £60 to a Seychelles planter for one. The Marquess of Ripon had also suggested to the British administrators on Mahé that several tortoises be brought to central Seychelles to ensure a safe breeding population there.

By 16th August, 1878, Captain Wharton was anchored off Zanzibar and wrote a report on his trip to Aldabra for Dr Gunther. He had, despite much searching, been able to find only one tortoise to send. 'Fishing-parties from the Seychelles are the enemies of the tortoise… and as they find the tortoises good to eat, they have nearly exterminated them.' However, he was hopeful that Aldabra's inhospitability would ensure its preservation. During his visit, there were no signs of any settlers, and he was sure he was safe in saying 'that Aldabra will never be inhabited regularly.' He assured Gunther that 'your mind may be at ease as regards any probability of Aldabra being inhabited; a more un-inviting place I never saw.'

Wharton went on: 'There is no soil, no sand even for planting coconuts, no water except in the cavities of the coral. Mosquitoes are intolerable…' Jules Cauvin of Mahé would probably have echoed these sentiments. The first lessee of Aldabra, he had made a settlement near West Channels and tried planting coconuts, but his venture failed.

On 30th September, 1878, the authorities on Mahé sent a ship themselves, the schooner *Flower of Jarrow*, with 'fishermen and labourers' to be stationed on the islands in the Aldabra group (Cosmoledo, Astove, Assumption and Aldabra). They also sent Sergeant Rivers, 'a very intelligent officer', to make a full report on these little-known islands. The sergeant produced a detailed account in December 1878.

He noted that 'this island seems to have been frequently visited by different parties as

remnants of different descriptions would seem to indicate.' Unlike Wharton he was able to locate a viable 'spring of excellent water' at Takamaka, which he estimated would give 'without running out at one time about thirty to forty barrels of water'. 'A kind of road' had been cut to the basin where the water was. He noted that in the south-east monsoon, boats could anchor off Picard 'at a place called "La Poste" and distinguished by a Cocoanut tree'. In the north-west monsoon they anchored off Grande Terre, at Cinq Cases 'where the "Tortoise" is generally caught.'

Turtles and fish were abundant and, because of the number of traces he found, he thought there were 'plenty' of tortoises, although he did not actually see any, 'the season being dry they remain hidden in holes…which makes it hard to find them.' 'I have never found any carcasses or shells of the tortoise,' he continues, 'and fishermen that have been there for a long time fishing told me that they had never found any except those that were killed for eating. It would also appear that some years ago some pigs were set loose on "Grande Ile" [Grande Terre] and did destroy a great many young tortoises, but as they were males they did not increase and must have been dead long ago. There are also a few goats found on "Ile Picard".' Man had really arrived on Aldabra!

Sergeant Rivers told his superiors that a settlement on Aldabra was very possible; there

was 'plenty of good ground upon which maize, sweet potatoes and other produce and cocoanuts could be planted. Goats thrive there also.' Even before Rivers' report had suggested that it was possible to settle on Aldabra, a lease of the atoll, along with Cosmoledo, Astove, and Assumption had been granted to Mr D'Offay, 'a Master Mariner of this Port' by November 1878. The Chief Civil Commissioner of Seychelles, C.S. Salmon, proposed to his superiors on Mauritius that these islands should continue to be leased. 'A house for the residence of the people could be made at Port Victoria and transported to Aldabra,' he wrote. 'Two or three men would suffice with the guardian and between them they could manage a short pirogue.' The only note of caution concerned the introduction of pigs, which would have to be prohibited, 'for, when loose, they are reported to destroy the young of the tortoises'.

D'Offay's lease lasted two years, during which time he probably earned an income from Aldabra by taking turtles, fish, and perhaps mangrove bark or timber. However, irrespective of the claims on Aldabra of Mr D'Offay and the British government, in 1879 plans were being made for a settlement there by a group of Norwegian hopefuls who evidently believed the atoll was still 'up for grabs'.

Between the 1860s and the 1880s, there was great Norwegian interest in Madagascar, to the extent that an almost regular liner service was established between the two countries. Although there were also hopes for settlement and trade, many of those who went to Madagascar were missionaries. The Norwegian Missionary Society had begun operations there in 1866.

Among the trading ventures, which were also intended to further missionary work, was an expedition led by Captain Ludwig Larsen, who established eight factories on the west coast of Madagascar, where he traded for two years until his London backers unexpectedly closed down their operations. Larsen, however, decided to stay on. His associates, who returned to Norway, wanted to organize a new expedition with the objective of settling Aldabra. The crew of a British man-of-war calling at Madagascar had somehow led them to believe that the atoll was uninhabited, unclaimed, and suitable for colonization.

While Larsen and those who remained in Madagascar struggled against deteriorating conditions, preparations went ahead in Norway and, by spring 1879, were almost complete. A galleas (a ship of the same construction as a galley, but larger and heavier) called *Debora* was purchased, but recruitment for the project was a problem. The organizers insisted that participants should be financially secure, physically fit, and with an interest in religion. The first two qualifications were the hardest to fulfil but, in July 1879, the *Debora* sailed from Bergen with a complement of forty-seven. Eighty-nine days later they arrived at Tulear in Madagascar to face great disappointment. Not only had those in Madagascar been unable to make any preparations, they now learned that it was almost certainly pointless to continue with the venture. The true, inhospitable nature of Aldabra was revealed to them. After much heart-searching, some decided to remain on Madagascar with Larsen, while the rest sailed on to South Africa and settled there; but none came to Aldabra.

From this time on, the British were to have trouble convincing others that Aldabra was theirs alone to dispose of. In 1882 the Civil Commissioner in Victoria was concerned by a report that Gaston Payet of Anse aux Pins, Mahé, had 'received a concession of Aldabra and Cosmoledo from the French government subject to his creating an establishment on the islands'. It is not clear if Aldabra was actually still leased, or what had become of Mr D'Offay at this time. Perhaps Aldabra had been abandoned so that the richer resources of the other islands included in the lease could be concentrated upon. Whatever the reason, when *HMS Griffon* visited Aldabra in 1888, they found it deserted. In 1889, however, there were yet more reports of the French government having leased Aldabra irrespective of British sovereignty. The potential lessee this time was Mr Minier, a former British government employee from Mauritius. 'Without therefore entering at present into the question of this man's behaviour,' wrote Governor Lees of Mauritius huffily to the Secretary of State for the Colonies, 'I venture to suggest to Your Lordship the advisability…of requesting the Lords of the Admiralty to give instructions to the Admiral on this Station to send a man-of-war to Aldabra.'

This was promptly done and, on 7th January 1890, Commander Edward Needham reported on a visit to Aldabra made by *HMS Reindeer*. There were now fifteen people on the island in the charge of Mr Lucien Pothier, 'having obtained permission from Mr Griffiths, the

Administrator of Seychelles, to catch turtles'. They took about 110 turtles a month but were 'prohibited from having anything to do with the Land Tortoises', and, in fact, only one tortoise had been seen while they were there. The men had arrived on Aldabra two months before Commander Needham's visit, on a schooner from Seychelles, and they expected to be taken off again four months later 'when the man Minier, whom they have heard of, may arrive'. They were living on fish and turtle only, and taking pity on them, Needham left them 150lbs of biscuit and 112lbs of oatmeal to vary their diet.

In March 1890, the British ambassador in Paris reported that the matter of Minier's supposed lease had been brought to the attention of the French government, but in 1891, Griffiths in Seychelles thought it prudent to lease the atoll again, this time to Mr Thomas James Spurs, for a period of five years. In June 1891, Griffiths writes that he 'took a new flagstaff and a couple of union Jacks and handed them to Mr. Spurs a British subject to whom the Aldabra group...are leased for five years — Mr. Spurs put up the new flag staff and flew the Jack at once.'

Spurs intended making the islands pay by taking 'upwards of 12,000 of the green or edible turtle, the meat of which he proposes to dry and ship'. The rent set was small, but Griffiths was pleased with his choice of lessee. In August 1891 he wrote to the Governor of Mauritius: 'I think the Government are fortunate in having secured Mr Spurs for a tenant... he is an observant man and a lover of nature, nor do I think that he is likely — to use an old and homely phrase — to kill the goose that lays the golden eggs by exhibiting that rapaciousness which has characterised the actions of others who have been there before him.' Spurs also had hopes for other 'industries' based in the Aldabra group. He took some Chinese from Mahé to prepare and dry sea cucumbers to make trepang, considered a delicacy in China, and intended to organize the collection of orchilla, or archil weed, a lichen which yields a red or violet dye, for export.

Despite Mr Spurs' presence, the Foreign Office in London was still keen that the Colonial Office should instigate 'some act of sovereignty...as a proof of British rights'. In February 1892, the Colonial Office was able to reassure the Foreign Office that such a gesture should no longer be necessary, since Mr Spurs now leased Aldabra, although they still thought it might be a good idea to send a naval vessel down to inspect the settlements. It seems that Griffiths did make an official visit and was able to report that all was well, news filtering back to Dr Gunther at the British Museum by February 1893 'that the protection of the Aldabra Tortoise has not been lost sight of'. However, Dr Gunther still had cause to feel 'sceptical as to the statements made by the present Lessee (Mr. Spurs) with regard to the number of individuals still found in Aldabra'.

Spurs was full of hope for the future of his venture, expecting to actually quadruple the figure he had estimated as a likely profit. In 1879 the islands had earned (presumably for Mr D'Offay) SR2,000/-. Spurs was therefore expecting some SR8,000/-. He thought the fishermen stationed on the islands would 'have no doubt a valuable cargo for the next and subsequent visits of the schooner'. All in all he was well pleased. 'In fact, the produce is

various, abundant and valuable and these Islands cannot fail to let well and to be a source of considerable revenue in the immediate future.'

There exists one curious reference in the records of Seychelles administration, to an incident in 1894 when a 'Mr Baty asks that he may go to Aldabra at his own expense… together with the man who reports discovering…treasure' on the island. Mr Harold Baty, owner of the Seychelles Lighterage Establishment, had encountered a Madagascan who claimed to know where a treasure was to be found on Aldabra. Mr Baty had some difficulty in securing the man's cooperation. In December 1894 he reports to Griffiths that in attempting to bring him into town for a meeting with the authorities, he had only 'managed to get the Malagache we are in want of as far as Mont Fleuri yesterday but his courage failed him and he "made tracks" for Anse Boileau'. We do not know what became of the recalcitrant Malagache or his treasure, though Mr Baty continued to interest himself in Aldabra, as we shall see.

In 1900 Mr Spurs applied for a renewal of his lease, due to expire on 31st May 1901. Yet again there was evidently concern about the welfare of the tortoises, and now even the hawksbill turtle, and some doubt as to whether Spurs could be trusted to obey the rules laid down for their protection. On 13th April 1901, Griffiths writes from Seychelles that 'Tortoises

*Below: A swathe of smooth sapphire and a bow of bright
turquoise: Main Channel seen from the air.*

*Opposite: Approximately sixty per cent of the lagoon's tidal flow passes
through Main Channel between Picard and Polymnie.*

and Hawksbill Turtles are expressly protected...though it is only fair to Mr Spurs to say that I have every reason to believe he has done his best to carry out these provisions of his Agreement.' However, he goes on to suggest that the lease be put up to tender by public auction in both England and Seychelles, and 'that an obligation be laid on the lessee to maintain on each of the Islands where the land tortoises and hawksbill turtles are to be found a guardian for the express purpose of seeing that there is no breach of these articles of the lease…'

The concerns regarding the lease prompted an official visit by *HMS Pomone*. A report made in July 1901 found Aldabra interesting from a scientific point of view, 'but it has little or no prospect of a good future from a commercial standpoint'. Maize, sweet potato, pumpkin, pawpaw and coconut trees planted by Mr Spurs were flourishing, and the goats he had introduced had 'thriven exceedingly…and abound in great numbers on Picard Island'. There were six fishermen in the employ of Mr Spurs based on Picard, along with five women and two children. The tortoises seemed to be properly protected and in no danger of dying out. There were traces of them all over Picard. Three were brought back to Mahé and put in a pen at Government House.

On 14th June 1901, Joseph Chamberlain, Secretary of State for the Colonies, had written

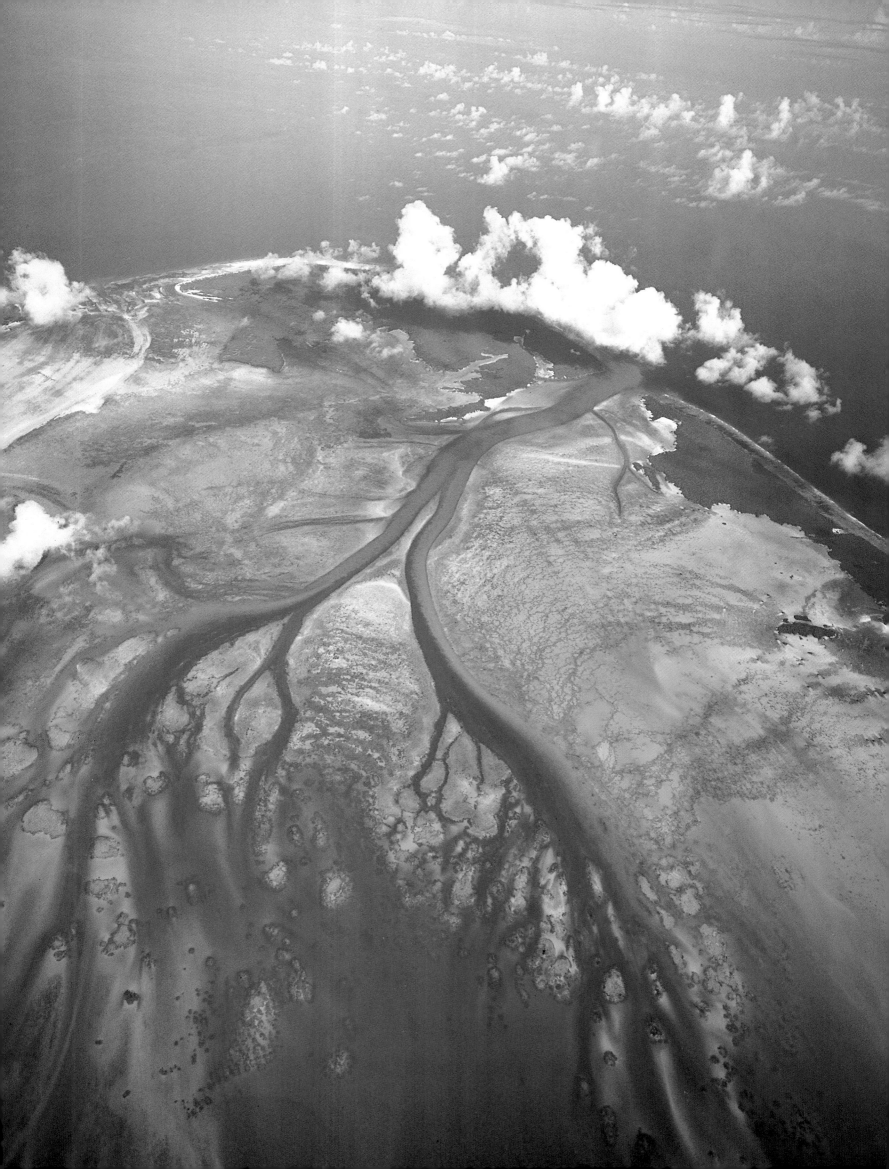

from Downing Street to E.B. Sweet-Escott, new Administrator (and later first Governor) of Seychelles, that 'confidential statements have been made to me to the effect that Mr J. Spurs, so far from protecting the land tortoises, actually sold large numbers of them, as many as twelve being taken away in one yacht'. A month later, Chamberlain dispatched a further minute concerning 'the alleged sale by Mr Spurs...of large numbers of land tortoises'. This prompted Griffiths to draw up a statement showing how many had been officially exported from Seychelles from 1890 to 30th August 1901. According to his table, none were legally exported until 1895 when Mr Spurs sent one to Mauritius and, the following year, sent two to Zanzibar. None were exported in the next two years, but in 1900 ten were sent to Bombay.

Downing Street seemed intent upon depriving Mr Spurs of his lease, however, especially since the wealth of the banking family the Rothschilds had now been dangled beneath their noses. Walter Rothschild, who had a 'well known interest...in gigantic tortoises', had offered to pay half the cost of the lease for any lessee who agreed to protect the tortoises, and 'do everything in his power to preserve those on Aldabra'. It was felt unnecessary to further investigate the case for or against Mr Spurs. In September 1901, London recommended that the lease be given to Baty, Bergne & Co., with interests in fishing and coconut planting at Aldabra, who had offered favourable terms. Mr Bergne had come to Seychelles in 1899 and formed a partnership with Harold Baty. The company's main concern was lighterage (loading and unloading of visiting vessels).

The lease was duly transferred and, on 16th December 1903, perhaps as a result of the death of Mr Baty in that year, was in turn transferred from them to 'Mr Adolphe d'Emmeroy' (Adolphe d'Emmerez de Charmoy), who owned a warehouse at the port, as well as Moyenne Island, and was somewhat of a local tycoon. He was the first car owner in Seychelles, and is reputed to have lit his cigars with bank notes. He made James Spurs his manager on Aldabra. In the same year, Seychelles ceased to be a dependency of Mauritius, and Aldabra was from this time administered directly from Victoria on Mahé.

During the lease of Mr Adolphe d'Emmerez de Charmoy, Aldabra had an outbreak of malaria in April 1908. A report from the Incorporated Liverpool School of Tropical Medicine, Liverpool University, suggested that a ship carrying infected persons, which had visited Aldabra, had brought a number of anopheline or malaria-carrying mosquitoes 'which bred copiously for a time in some favourable spot, and then died out'. In 1930, Dr J. Bradley, Chief Medical Officer, examined labourers returning from Aldabra and found them to be suffering from malaria, suggesting that the atoll had a population of anopheline mosquitoes which periodically flared up. However, no outbreaks have been reported since.

Aldabra was increasingly attracting the notice of naturalists and collectors. A Mauritian who had lived in Seychelles for over twenty years, and was creator of Mahé's Botanical Gardens and Director of the Botanic Station (1901–1921 and 1924–1934), Mr Rivaltz Dupont, spent two months researching on Aldabra in 1906, and published his report in 1907. One of the most glamorous visitors was the Earl of Crawford aboard his 1700-ton yacht *Valhalla*, the 'first ship fitted with the Brougham patent electrical steering-gear'! As Crawford put it, for many years he had had to 'live in close communion with two inseparable hangers-on; the one rheumatism, the other asthma'. He found that a life at sea in tropical climes was good for his health and made several round-the-world voyages. Himself a trustee of the British Museum, it was suggested to him by a fellow trustee that he take the opportunity to collect specimens for the museum. On his voyages, he was accompanied by naturalist Michael J. Nicoll, a member of the British Ornithologists Union. On the third round-the-world trip, during which they visited Aldabra and went aground on Assumption, the entomologist E.G.B. Meade-Waldo was also aboard.

Nicoll obviously had a wonderful time. 'The accommodation on board is palatial,' he enthused about the *Valhalla*, and a crew of about 65, including 'officers, engineers, and stewards' was available to tend to their passengers' every need. 'A better or more beautiful yacht could not be imagined,' said Nicoll. The *Valhalla* sailed from Cowes on 8th November 1905 and spent 13th to 16th March 1906 at Aldabra. Like many before and since, the *Valhalla* was to experience the ferocity of Aldabra's tides and currents, and dragged her anchor. No damage was done, however. Nicoll saw no tortoises, which he believed were confined to a small area in the north, but he says 'the Hon Walter Rothschild rents the island...and protects the tortoises as well as a peculiar species of ibis, so that it is to be hoped that these interesting creatures may long hold their own.' At this time, many coconuts had been planted and the settlement consisted of 'a few wooden huts, inhabited by negroes, who, under the supervision of an overseer, work in the cocoanut plantations and at turtle-catching and curing'.

As if Aldabra was not already facing enough threats, there was also talk now of mining the phosphates there. However, the report from the Imperial Institute, London, on coral sent from Aldabra, concluded that the phosphates there were not of sufficient value to export, although 'the inferior specimens might be of value locally for manurial purposes'.

In 1908 the Percy Sladen Trust Expedition visited Aldabra aboard the *Sealark*. William Percy Sladen was a self-taught English zoologist. The expeditions were led by Professor Stanley Gardiner, and their exhaustive reports were published in the Transactions of the Linnaean Society of London. J.C.F. Fryer of Cambridge University made a collection of insects in 1908.

Despite all this scientific interest, it still seemed to be touch and go for the tortoises. On 26th May 1909, Governor Davidson of Seychelles passed on a report from de Charmoy that the tortoises were 'in danger of extinction owing to the depredations of the cranes which are alleged to destroy the young'.

The next lessees of the Aldabra group were a company called Biggerstaff & Co. of London, who bought the lease from de Charmoy in 1914. In December of that year, their representative, Mr Brownjohn, was in Victoria to put his 'clients' title on a proper footing'. The main interest of Biggerstaffs was the guano on the islands, and Mr Brownjohn was in search of expert advice as to the 'quantity and quality of the guano deposits'. After 1879, only approximately 50,000 to 100,000 tons of high-grade guano was thought to be left on the outer

Camp of labourers at Aldabra-Island October 1907

A. d'Emmerez de Charmoy, lessee

islands. In 1916, Rivaltz Dupont was, fortunately for posterity, able to advise that 'no marketable guano is found at Aldabra'.

In the meantime, of course, there was war in Europe, and its effects were felt as far afield as Aldabra. The Germans had stationed one of their new, fast battleships, the *Königsberg*, in the Indian Ocean to carry out, in the event of war, a privateering campaign, preying on merchant ships plying from South and East Africa, to Suez, as well as threatening shipping lines to Australia, Singapore, Java, Calcutta and Bombay, 'ready to murder the ships of the merchant fleet as a spider murders flies'.

The *Königsberg* was just seven years old at the outbreak of war. She was longer and slimmer than those British ships which were initially sent to track her down. She displaced just 3,400 tons, whereas the flagship of the English admiral in charge of seeking her displaced 5,700 tons.

The crew of the *Königsberg* learned of the outbreak of war on 5th August 1914. The very next day, despite being short of coal, they captured the *City of Winchester* with a large cargo of tea. A rendezvous was arranged between the *Königsberg* and a collier at Aldabra for September 1914. The atoll was sufficiently remote to ensure privacy, but the exposed anchorage made the transfer of coal difficult. The *Königsberg* was off Zanzibar later that month and she sank a British cruiser before hiding in the delta of the Rufiji River on the East African coast. The German command were anxious to refuel the *Königsberg* and sent a steamer, *Rubens*, in the hope of making another rendezvous off Aldabra in April 1915. However, the *Königsberg* never arrived. She had been trapped in the Rufiji delta by a British blockade since October 1914.

In an attempt to locate the cruiser, the *Rubens* sent a wireless message. The British picked it up and were able to intercept her in Manza Bay where she was run aground in April 1914. Meanwhile, on Mahé, the authorities were disturbed by a coded radio message overheard by a ship passing through Seychelles waters, which included the call sign of the *Königsberg*. They were unable to decode the message locally, and for all they knew in Seychelles, the dreaded battle cruiser was headed straight for the colony. Ships in the area were told to go into Port Victoria for shelter.

The local version of events is that a Seychelles fishing boat calling at Aldabra saw the *Königsberg* itself at anchor in the lagoon and hurried back to Mahé to report it. What seems more likely is that they saw the *Rubens*, a smaller vessel. Confusion was probably compounded because the *Rubens* was pretending to be a neutral Norwegian vessel called the *Krönberg*. When the fishermen returned to Mahé, they would have found everyone anticipating the arrival of the *Königsberg* and, given the similarity of the two ships' names, the *Krönberg* quite easily became the *Königsberg*. In fact, the *Königsberg* was kept at bay on the Rufiji River until she was finally sunk in July 1915.

Our next picture of Aldabra comes from a report written by Rivaltz Dupont in July 1916, when the resources of Aldabra were considered to be: '1) Turtle and its derivatives 2) Salt fish 3) Mangrove bark 4) Copra 5) Maize'. The new lessees were urged to develop these 'industries', establish new ones, and encourage the growth of a permanent population on the atoll. Looking to the future, Dupont pointed out that, since cotton grew well on Aldabra, 'should a small community with women and children labour be established at Aldabra, the culture of cotton which necessitates hand-picking of the crop should be attempted.' Other suggested crops were sisal, citrus trees, vanilla and perfume plants. There was room for about 5,000 coconut palms and 'if a supply of labour were established at Aldabra the exploitation of the mangrove forest could be carried on more cheaply'.

The goats had 'instinctively abandoned the less hospitable districts for the green pasture', and although turtles, at least, were still considered very numerous, 'many fishing vessels come over from Mahé and cannot be controlled in their work of destroying turtles, tortoises and goats...'

Hopes for an agricultural station on the atoll were quickly quashed by the government as being 'Utopian' and impossible to finance in 'a small Colony whose revenue is only able to meet present demands with care, and where the population is so impatient of any increased taxation'.

In 1922, the partnership of Biggerstaffs was dissolved and Mr Thomas Lloyd Cyril d'Arcy Leaver, a former partner, formed a new company called the Seychelles Guano Company and

Below: The German battleship Königsberg *in the Indian Ocean at the outbreak of war, refuelled at Aldabra. It was trapped by a British blockade in the Rufiji delta and eventually sunk.*

applied for a transfer of the lease. This new company was fifty per cent owned by the Niger Company who, by April 1922, claimed to have already spent some £35,000 on the Aldabra project. Heavy expenses had been incurred due to the war. The lease transfer was approved that month.

A year later, the new company's agent, Mr Sewell, was established in Seychelles and their schooner, the *Meredith A. White* (500 tons), had arrived with a cargo of goods to enable them to open 'a small trading business'. It was expected that the *Meredith A. White* would trade between Seychelles, East Africa, Madagascar and Mauritius under the supervision of Mr Sewell.

In 1926 the Seychelles Guano Company was still leasing Aldabra, and the government of Seychelles recommended that, on the expiry of the present lease (30th August 1931), they should be given a further thirty-year lease at a cost of SR6000/- per year rent. The governor felt the company had 'made a genuine effort to carry out its obligations', despite the lease having proved more of a liability than a source of income to date. 'I very much doubt if we could ever obtain an equally satisfactory lessee,' he concluded.

Dupont made another visit to Aldabra that year, and found that 'not much use is made of the natural resources of that island except regarding the production of calipee and salt fish....

Timber from the mangrove swamps near Ile Verte is being exploited by fourteen sawyers and bushmen....A little Indian corn, castor oil and sweet potatoes is [sic] grown by the lessees. The coconut palms numbering about 1500 and planted thirty-one years ago by Mr J. Spurs at Picard are well looked after...the Camp, Prison & Hospital accommodation left nothing to be desired...and it appears that no fine or imprisonment was inflicted on the labourers by the late or present managers. The sanitary condition of the island was good.'

In 1928, the Seychelles Guano Company became the Seychelles Company. Dupont visited Aldabra again in 1929 with the governor Sir George Honey, and in his report on the trip, expressed concern that 'the sea and land birds of Aldabra...were being destroyed by the labourers and are rapidly becoming extinct'.

In July 1933, the Seychelles Company was trying to renegotiate its rent. Dupont, asked for his opinion, was unsympathetic. 'There is no reason to decrease the rental, which is already low (SR2,000),' he wrote in October. In December, the matter having been discussed by the Executive Council of the colony, the company was granted a renewal of its lease for three more years, but conditions remained unaltered.

By 1938, the rent for the lease of Aldabra and Cosmoledo, negotiated between the governor Sir Arthur Grimble and local manager Marcel Lemarchand was SR4,600/- but the company seems to have been struggling. The outbreak of the Second World War made matters worse. In May 1940, they asked for a waiver of Article 5 of their lease, under which they promised to 'remove from the said Islands and export from the Colony a minimum of 2,000 tons of guano per annum' for the duration of the war, since they could not find the ships to carry it. Despite the additional difficulties, they still applied for a two-year renewal of their lease, on the same conditions, in September 1940. Again they were granted the lease, although the council was sufficiently concerned about the turtle stocks to have considered a total ban on the exploitation of sea turtle.

It was the question of the turtles which finally stung the Seychelles Company into written protest at the conditions imposed on it by the local council. In the end, the government on Mahé had to give up any ideas about the conservation of the turtles because the pressures of the war on the colony meant they were very short of meat. They asked the Seychelles Company to 'ship to Mahé not less than 1,000 live turtles a year'. They were no longer allowed to kill and dry turtles on Aldabra for export. The company declared these conditions impossible. They pointed out that their boat could only carry sixty live turtles at once, given good weather, and that if they attempted to increase that number, some twenty-five per cent of the animals would die en route. They added that Aldabra was of little use to them, having no guano worth exporting, and producing 'scarcely anything besides turtles, which are of little commercial interest'.

For their part, the men on Mahé explained that they needed live turtles shipped to Mahé because it being war time, 'the local Indian Forces have made exhaustive inroads into the resources of poultry and tanker crews and European personnel of the Forces have looked to the local market for meat', and so 'the introduction...of a larger supply of turtle and goats

from Aldabra appeared to be desirable'. The Seychelles Company seem to have struggled to make something out of Aldabra and Cosmoledo until 1945, when commercial leasing of Aldabra was suspended for a period of ten years. In February 1955, it was again leased, for a period of thirty years, to Mr Harry Savy.

Under the terms of his lease, South Island (Grande Terre) was to be kept as a reserve, without human settlement, where all animal life was to be respected and no new animals could be introduced. The lessor was still allowed to take up to 500 green turtles a year, but no eggs. There was no control over the cutting of mangrove wood, or the taking of fish and shellfish. There was, however, some control over rock quarrying, timber felling (other than mangrove), and land clearance. The lessee was to be 'the guardian and protector of all wild life and all the resources of the Islands' and ensure that 'no wild birds, tortoises or other animals are molested'. These more stringent conditions were probably inserted because of the visit of the famous marine biologist Commander Jacques Cousteau to Aldabra in 1953, and his subsequent application for the lease of the atoll in order to make it a 'wild life reserve, and tropical research centre'. This application, however, was turned down.

Since 1901, the turtles on Aldabra had been protected to some degree by fisheries ordinances. In 1948 the Acting Director of Agriculture, Felix Durocher Yvon, was sent with

F.D. Ommanney, a fisheries expert, to report on the numbers of green turtles in the region of Aldabra. As a result, new regulations for their protection were brought in. Tortoises, except those on Grande Terre, were still only protected under the Customs Management Ordinance, prohibiting their export. In 1941, five species of Aldabran birds were protected under an act, and the number rose to twelve in the Plumage Birds (Exportation) Ordinance of 1947. The atoll itself, however, remained unprotected, except by the provisions of the new lease.

As we have seen, Aldabra's unique wildlife had had several brushes with potential disaster over the years. None was to come closer than that which now loomed on the horizon. In 1962, the British government commissioned a secret military survey of Aldabra and other western Indian Ocean islands, in search of a potential military base in the region. The findings prompted the choice of Aldabra by the Ministry of Defence.

By 1964 the newspapers had caught wind of the plan and, in April 1965, *The Times* of London reported that Aldabra, Diego Garcia and Cocos-Keeling were being considered as sites for a future Anglo-American military base. The probable impact of such development on these relatively unspoilt and little-known islands was of concern to the Southern Zone Research Committee of the Royal Society, in London. The British Broadcasting Corporation was considering building a radio transmitter on Aldabra and was sending a team of

*Below left: Modern communications have reached Aldabra
providing the workers at the research station with instant access
to the outside world.*

*Below right: Using devices such as this, the meteorological
station gathers data such as hours of sunshine.*

technicians and surveyors to examine the site. The Ministry of Defence and other ministries were keen to have the atoll surveyed for their own purposes, and a joint expedition was formed. The Royal Society, therefore, requested that two scientists, Dr D.R. Stoddart of the Department of Geography, University of Cambridge, and Dr C.A. Wright of the Department of Zoology, British Museum (Natural History), should accompany it. This request was granted.

In December 1965, before this expedition departed, the British government, despite opposition within the colony of Seychelles, had taken the step of forming a new colony, the British Indian Ocean Territory, or BIOT, which consisted of all the islands in the region considered suitable for military bases; that is, Aldabra, Farquhar, Desroches and Chagos (taken from the territory of the colony of Mauritius). It looked as though Aldabra must already be doomed.

Drs Stoddart and Wright spent two weeks on Aldabra in August 1966 with the survey party. On returning to Britain, a 'Report on the Conservation of Aldabra' was written by Dr Stoddart, and considered by the Royal Society's Southern Zone Research Committee. Besides establishing the great importance of Aldabra as a scientific site, the report also suggested ways of minimizing the impact of a military base on the wildlife of the atoll.

*Below: To reach the field station at Cinq Cases,
it is necessary to cross the lagoon by boat, then wade
the last few hundred metres to dry land.*

The proposed base was to include a 4,500-metre runway and staging-post buildings on Grande Terre, a dam across Main Channel to create a harbour facility for tankers, and a road from Main Channel across Passe Houareau to Grande Terre. The dreadful implications for the wildlife were obvious. The runway and buildings would obliterate an area where thousands of tortoises lived, and the aircraft would be a threat to birds in flight (and vice versa). The dam would affect tides and water circulation in the lagoon, and thus the wading birds, mangroves and other life dependent upon it. The road would cut through frigate and booby colonies and make it easier for predators established on Picard or Grande Terre to reach colonies of white-throated rail on Malabar and Polymnie. Also, there was the great probability of the introduction of alien species, pollution, and the risk of a major disaster such as fire.

The report was passed on to the Ministry of Defence, and the Royal Society organized a conference of interested parties in January 1967. Representatives of national and international scientific and conservation organizations attended, including the National Academy of Sciences and the Smithsonian Institute.

The conference fully supported the Royal Society's case for preserving Aldabra and proposed the speedy establishment of a nature reserve and research station there. The

building of a military base on Aldabra was agreed to be a potential biological disaster.

An expedition was now planned by the Royal Society itself, and an Aldabra Sub-Committee was formed to handle matters. A Society press notice of 22nd February 1967 voiced its 'considerable concern' over the government proposals and made an announcement about the expedition. In March, the Under-Secretary of State for the Royal Air Force referred in the House of Commons to the growing concern about Aldabra, and assured the Royal Society that their arguments against the base would be fully considered. He added that if the government's plan for Aldabra did go ahead, every effort would be made to minimize its impact, and a research facility would be provided.

A 'Memorandum on Aldabra' was, meanwhile, in preparation which stated the case for total preservation of the atoll. Approved by the Natural Environment Research Council and the British Museum (Natural History), it was circulated to the Ministry of Defence and other departments. In May 1967, the Society also took an unusual step in sending its president, Professor P.M.S. Blackett, with a delegation, directly to the Minister of Defence. The minister promised a decision on Aldabra within twelve months.

Now the battle for Aldabra was truly in the public domain. Opinions flew, editorials were written, and questions were asked. The proposal to build a base on Aldabra was called 'entirely indefensible'. During August 1967, *The Times* of London was the focal point of the debate when Sir Tufton Beamish and others commented in a letter on the practical difficulties of building a base on Aldabra's notoriously difficult terrain. Other contributors on the subject included Viscount Ridley, Sir Julian Huxley, Professor Wynne-Edwards and Sir Dermot Boyle. The issue was featured in *Nature, The Spectator, New Scientist, New Statesman, Science, The New York Times, Oryx,* and *Time.* The topic was further debated in the House of Commons and, in Seychelles, the Seychelles People's United Party mounted a campaign against the plans.

Despite all this, however, in August 1967, just after the Royal Society expedition began, the decision was actually taken to go ahead with building the base. This was later admitted by the Minister of Defence, but when questioned in the House of Commons on 25th October as to whether a decision had been taken, he said that he could make no statement. Later the same day, Mr Tam Dalyell, Labour MP for West Lothian, raised the matter again and followed up the debate with a series of detailed Parliamentary Questions directed at the minister concerned. By 7th November, Mr Dalyell had tabled over fifty questions on Aldabra, so that the Speaker ruled that no more questions on the subject could be put by him. Over a dozen MPs took up the cause and twenty-five questions were answered between 15th and 21st November. In the House of Lords, Lord Ridley announced that he would be seeking a debate on Aldabra at the end of November. A television documentary filmed on Aldabra by Tony Beamish, called *Island in Danger* was broadcast by the BBC on 29th October and followed by a televised debate. Support for the Royal Society's cause became overwhelming, both among the public and the scientific and conservation establishment.

Then, as suddenly as the crisis had blown up, it was over. On 18th November 1967, it was announced that the pound sterling would be devalued, and that there would no longer be a British military presence east of Suez. On 22nd November the government announced that it would not go ahead with its plans to build a base on Aldabra. However, the Minister of Defence, Mr Healey, did not rule out the possibility of building the base when economic conditions improved.

Meanwhile, the Royal Society's Aldabra Research Committee was still working towards the establishment of a research station. A site on Picard was chosen and surveyed in August 1968; building work beginning in October 1969. The buildings were mostly complete by early 1971, and the formal opening of the Aldabra Research Station took place on 30th June 1971. The following month, the lessee of Aldabra, Mr Savy, agreed to give up the remainder of his lease to the Royal Society, although, due to administrative problems, the lease did not officially become theirs until April 1976.

Aldabra was returned from BIOT to the colony of Seychelles in June 1976, shortly after which Seychelles itself became an independent republic. Intensive research work continued at the station, the results of which confirmed the atoll's significance and importance in the field of ecological and evolutionary studies. A secure future needed to be guaranteed for

Aldabra in respect of both its physical protection and financial support. It was decided to form an independent, self-funded charitable trust, Seychelles Islands Foundation, to conserve and manage Aldabra in perpetuity. This was established by presidential decree on 2nd February 1979. The Chairman of the new Board of Trustees, Dr Maxime Ferrari, visited Aldabra and unveiled a plaque which reads in English and French, 'Aldabra, wonder of nature, given to humanity by the people of the Republic of Seychelles'. The United Nations proclaimed Aldabra a World Heritage Site in 1982.

It is, therefore, to be hoped that Aldabra is finally safe from possible destruction at the hands of man, and that in years to come, privileged visitors may still be able to witness the setting sun there, as Ommanney described it in 1952, 'sending searchlights through the casuarinas, quivering veils and curtains of golden light…the moon sailed high and pale in an opalescent sky dotted with frigate birds still wheeling high above Aldabra'.

2

PLANET ALDABRA

DR PHIL PLUMMER

'The ocean throwing its waters over the broad reef appears an invincible, all-powerful enemy, yet we see it resisted and even conquered by means which at first seem most weak and inefficient....Yet these low, insignificant coral islets stand and are victorious.'
Journal of Researches into the Geology and Natural History of the various countries visited
by HMS Beagle
Charles Darwin

Above: Much of the interior of Aldabra is extremely difficult to explore on foot because of the champignon rock and almost impenetrable vegetation.

THE ALDABRA THAT YOU SEE NOW, THE world's largest raised atoll, is the ornate coralline cap of a conical volcanic mountain — technically a guyot or seamount — that lurks beneath the waters of the western Indian Ocean from a truly abyssal sea floor, over 4,000 metres down and comprising some of the oldest oceanic crust on the planet. The seamount lies in the southern part of the Somali Basin, the oldest part of the Indian Ocean.

Oceans have come and gone over the past billion years of geological history as the continental land masses have constantly drifted over the Earth's crust, sliding over the molten upper mantle on the backs of gigantic plates. Repeatedly, the continents have combined and separated, and some 275 million years ago, at the close of the coaly Carboniferous age, they had united to form the single, V-shaped megacontinent of Pangaea (meaning 'all lands'). Between Pangaea's wings lay Tethys, a seaway that, when later extended by rifting, divided Pangaea into two supercontinents: northern Laurasia, made up of North America, Europe and Asia; and southern Gondwana, composed of South America, Antarctica, Australia, Africa and India. The Seychelles microcontinent lay central to Gondwana, jammed, with Madagascar, between Africa and India.

The Somali Basin formed slowly, over a period of perhaps 150 million years, as a titanic rift that eventually split the Gondwana supercontinent into East and West blocks about 160 million years ago, in the middle of the geological age known as the Jurassic and famous for its dinosaurs. A series of volcanoes central to this rift spewed out basaltic lavas that, being heavier than the granites of the adjacent continents, depressed the ever-widening rift that slowly pushed East and West Gondwana apart. Eventually that depressed rift — the Somali Basin — was flooded from the north with waters from ancient Tethys and the proto-Indian Ocean was born. After some forty-five million years, towards the middle of the Cretaceous geological period, this ocean-forming process ceased. The positions of the then East and West Gondwanas are still marked today by the coastlines of western Madagascar on one side, and Tanzanian East Africa on the other. The granitic Seychelles split off from Madagascar, along with India, some twenty million years later, about ninety-five million years ago. But the seamount that is Aldabra, and its smaller neighbour Assumption, both formed later, although just when is uncertain, for their foundations have never been sampled by drill-bit or dredge. Nevertheless, similar nearby features have been dated and thus Aldabra's age can be estimated.

The Formation of Aldabra

The Comoros Islands are a chain of emergent seamounts oriented roughly east-west and situated some 400 kilometres south-west of Aldabra. The largest and most westerly island, Grande Comore, still has an active volcano, the Kartala crater. However, the further east you go in the chain, the longer it is since the volcanoes died out. As the islands become progressively older they display less topographic relief, but greater development of surrounding coral reefs. Mayotte, the easternmost and oldest island of the Comoros chain, is an ever-diminishing extinct volcanic peak in a reef-encircled lagoon.

Beyond Mayotte the pattern of islands swings north-eastwards, parallel to the Madagascan coast, through the shallowly submerged banks of Castor and Geyser, and tiny remnant Iles Glorieuses where the fiery creation ceased some ten million years ago. From there, the ever-older volcanic chain continues north, as indicated by a series of atolls, including Cosmoledo. This line of islands marks the trace of the Earth's crust migrating over a 'hotspot' of magma within the mantle. By comparing this Comoros Hotspot trace with other well-dated traces, such as that through Réunion-Mauritius-Saya de Mahla, it can be estimated that the Aldabra/Assumption seamount complex, which lies just west of Cosmoledo, formed about the same time as the hotspot outlet some twenty million years ago; or geologically during the earliest Miocene epoch of the Tertiary period.

The tendency for islands within volcanic chains to display diminishing topographic relief with increasing development of encircling reefs was noted by Charles Darwin during the famed voyage of the *HMS Beagle* between 1832 and 1836. Knowing also that corals grew only in shallow waters of tropical oceans, down to some sixty metres, Darwin deduced that corals forming atoll reefs amid the deep oceans required a substrate on which to grow and, as early as 1839, he correctly suggested that submerged volcanic craters provided that substrate. Darwin was unaware, however, of the mechanism for the submergence of the

volcanoes, namely the cooling and contraction of the seamounts as the migrating Earth's crust dragged them away from the volcanic outlet of mantle hotspots.

Inherent in Darwin's model of atoll formation is the implication that, with reef growth keeping pace with gradual substrate subsidence, great thicknesses of coralline rock can underlie present-day mid-oceanic atolls. Indeed, geophysical studies of Aldabra atoll indicate the top of the volcanic seamount to lie beneath at least 500 metres of reef rock.

So it has long been recognized that the subsidence of seamounts enables atolls to form. But the amount of submergence, in relation to average sea level, is not necessarily due to tectonic subsidence alone. A rise in sea level produces, in the geological record of the reef, the equivalent effect of tectonic subsidence. The growth of atolls, therefore, is closely related to the interplay of tectonic subsidence with sea level fluctuations; and during ice ages sea level fluctuations can be dramatic.

Over the past two million years — the period defined geologically as the Pleistocene — the planet's climate has fluctuated significantly. Five major cycles of climatic cooling have occurred to which, each time, the polar ice-caps responded by advancing towards the equator. The result of all that extra ice locked up in the expanding ice-caps was a drop in sea level, perhaps by as much as 150 metres below that of the present day. However, each of

these five Pleistocene ice ages — the Donau, Gunz, Mindel, Riss and Wurm — were themselves composed of mini climatic cycles. Sea level changes throughout the Pleistocene have, therefore, been anything but stable, and it was within this setting that today's visible atoll developed at Aldabra.

The Pleistocene Geology of Aldabra

On Aldabra there are no outcrops of the contact layer between the volcanic seamount and the capping coral reef sediments. Also, of the exposed rocks, only the uppermost layers provide material adequate for age dating. Thus the actual age of the oldest exposed rocks can only be estimated, and they are widely believed to be of middle to late Pleistocene age; about one million years old. It is quite possible, however, that an older sequence, perhaps of Pliocene age — between two and five million years old — lies between the oldest exposed rocks and the underlying seamount volcanic rocks. Only by drilling a borehole could such a supposition be tested.

   The stratigraphy of Aldabra is complex; the character of the rocks changing dramatically over only short distances. The different types are all carbonate sediments of biological origin derived from prolific molluscan (shelly), algal, and coralline growth. The observed

arrangement of rock layers has resulted from the interaction between this carbonate production during periods of high sea level, and destructive or eroding processes that were prevalent during periods of low sea level, which include, in order of relative importance, mechanical, biological and chemical erosion.

The island of Esprit, situated in the western part of the lagoon and which rises to some eight metres above the present sea level, is believed to contain the oldest rocks exposed at Aldabra. The Esprit Limestone comprises thick beds of fine sand-sized material, which, in some places, is much coarser and forms beds of shell grit. Such rocks typically accumulate in shallow, sub-tidal environments (less than twenty metres deep) that are dominated by wave action. These limestones have been tightly cemented and fossils are poorly preserved. Nevertheless, bivalves form nearly ninety per cent of the molluscan fauna with many showing evidence of death from being bored into by the carnivorous natica snail. Corals do not occur often in these layers. Towards the top of the rock sequence, a different shelly fauna indicates a shallower, more sheltered environment, with somewhat restricted water circulation in which mangroves flourished.

The continuing drop in relative sea level resulted in these rocks being stranded above sea level, thereby allowing chemical solution weathering to dissolve pockets of the sediment, leaving jagged-edged pits and cavities that characterize surfaces known as karst topography. The dissolved carbonate was redeposited elsewhere as a cement binding the loose sediment into limestone rock.

On the highest of the karstified Esprit Limestone occurs a layer of two metres maximum thickness comprising very distinctive laminated, fine-grained sediments, cemented with phosphate rather than with carbonate. Later erosion concentrated the phosphates as conglomerates or red-brown oolites in solution cavities (oolites are rocks composed of sub-spherical particles, called ooliths, that have grown by accretion around a nucleus, such as a sand grain). The source of the phosphate is presumed to have been guano (from ground-nesting seabirds) that accumulated in hollows, or perhaps caves, although the island topography at this time is unknown.

On Picard and in the West Channels area there is a three-metre-thick well-bedded calcarenite (i.e., sandstone of biological origin). The characteristics of this rock type suggest that it was formed by the accumulation of particles in a wave-dominated environment. To the west, the calcarenite contains progressively more coral and algal fragments, and eventually corals fossilized in growth positions. Also contained within these calcarenites are pebbles eroded from the distinctive Esprit Phosphorite, indicating that the Picard Calcarenite was formed later.

The upper layer of the Picard Calcarenite contains abundant land snails and other terrestrial fossils, such as tortoise bones (including full skeletons), bird bones, crocodile teeth and plant rootlets. The additional presence of occasional shark and pufferfish teeth is thought to have resulted from such species dying after becoming stranded on a beach.

In places, the main calcarenite is capped by a ten-centimetre-thick brown, porcelain-like

Below: The present-day surface morphology of Aldabra is the
result of interaction between weathering processes active since
early into the last glacial period, some 120,000 years ago.

limestone that contains ostracods (small crustaceans), foraminifera (microscopic organisms), algae, fragments of corals and molluscs, and locally abundant land snails. The surface of this porcellaneous limestone also contains burrows and plant rootlet tubes.

The Picard Calcarenite, therefore, appears to represent an accumulation of bioclastic sand (broken shells and corals) that developed behind an active reef and eventually rose to three metres above sea level as a sand cay. The presence of tortoises, crocodiles, land snails and plants suggest the cay was vegetated and quite big, a contention supported by a similar calcarenite outcropping along the southern coast some twenty-seven kilometres east of Picard that was formed at the same time as the Picard Calcarenite. The surface of the western end of this extensive cay was perhaps a shallow dune field where, between the dunes, standing bodies of fresh water occurred, which produced the capping porcellaneous limestones.

The dominant rock formation to be seen on the Aldabra islands, with the exception of small Polymnie, is the Takamaka Limestone. Only on Picard, however, is the close relationship evident between these limestones and the underlying Picard Calcarenite. The contact between them indicates that no period of subaerial exposure separates the two types, but rather that a change in the conditions of deposition occurred due to a rise in sea level which flooded the Picard sand cay.

The Takamaka Limestone comprises generally mud-sized sediment in the south-west of the atoll, while elsewhere sand- and even gravel-sized sediment predominates. The limestones are characterized by abundant calcareous red algae, especially benthic (bottom-dwelling) species. Other fossils are uncommon but include corals and, more rarely, molluscs, which generally occur in the east and south-east of the atoll. Both massive and branched corals are present while marine snails, notably trochids, dominate over bivalves. The majority of molluscs, however, are associated with hard, weathered substrates, indicating that they bored into the rock at a later date after its formation.

The general paucity of corals and molluscs suggests that the environment at that time was stressful. It is possible that the sea level rise that flooded the Picard sand cay and formed the five-metre-deep Takamaka platform resulted from an interglacial period (i.e., a time between two ice-ages) during which temperatures did not rise significantly.

The upper surface of the Takamaka Limestone is generally flat, but with pits and cavities, having been bored into by molluscs and chemically weathered. A buff-coloured fossil soil fills the cavities and here and there forms a thin crusty layer. It is apparent, therefore, that deposition of the limestones ceased when sea level once again dropped and exposed the extensive Takamaka platform. During this emergence, cliffs were eroded into the limestone

*Below: Fossil corals in growth positions such as these
have been dated between 136,000 and 118,000 years old.*

in the east and south-east, while shallow channels meandered towards the south-eastern and south-western parts of the atoll.

A brief flooding of the weathered Takamaka platform followed and a series of sand banks and beaches developed, principally at the eastern end of the atoll. Often the internal structure within these sands has been destroyed by the subsequent burrowing action of molluscs and crabs. In places the fauna contained within any single deposit range from distinctly marine at the base to terrestrial at the top. It is possible that these calcarenites emerged to form perhaps a single cay over the eastern portion of the atoll.

The outer rim of Aldabra is formed by the youngest sequence of rocks, known as the Aldabra Limestone. Fossil corals found in growth positions within these limestones, between two and seven metres above the present sea level, have been dated at between 136,000 and 118,000 years old. This coincides with the interglacial period between the Riss and Wurm ice ages, the latter of which the planet has been steadily emerging from for only the past 11,000 years. The climatic warming during the Riss-Wurm interglacial period induced the sea level to rise steadily by some ten metres before the ensuing Wurm glacial period once again plunged the planet into an icy grip and resulted in a drop in sea levels.

The Aldabra Limestone is formed primarily from fossil corals in a matrix that ranges from very fine particles to quite large, rubble-sized pieces. Abundant corals and molluscs are generally well preserved, the former often in growth positions and the latter frequently retaining their original colouration. However, there is considerable variation across the atoll, perhaps as a result of seasonal south-east/north-west monsoonal changes in climate, as is the case today.

For example, around the rim, branching corals (especially acropora) dominate the south, south-east and north-east coasts while faviid corals (stony corals such as brain coral) dominate the north-west coast. Changes also occur from the rim in towards the centre of the atoll, where there is not only a general decrease in the abundance of corals but also a replacement of branching corals by faviid forms. Additionally, in the inner atoll rocks, calcarenites rich in fossil molluscs dominate the north-western portion, with some 400 species recognized, while algae-rich calcarenites dominate the southern and eastern areas. Finally, differences in rock characteristics also resulted from a shallowing of the sea and some localities show evidence of periods of emergence, with even encrusted and bored subaerial hardgrounds (soils cemented by the precipitation of limestone from ground water evaporation), amid the Aldabra Limestone. These periods are likely to have arisen from fluctuations in the rate of sea level rise during the interglacial period.

In general, then, the Aldabra Limestone, although complex in its internal arrangement, formed on a broad, coral-rimmed platform in shallow waters, with a maximum depth of perhaps ten metres. The abundance of animal life testifies to normal marine salinities and good water circulation, while variations across the atoll perhaps resulted from a monsoonal climate similar to that of today.

Deposition of the Aldabra Limestone ceased when the climate was plunged into the grip of the last Pleistocene glacial period — the Wurm — which started some 120,000 years ago and ended a mere 11,000 years ago. During that time, sea level is estimated to have dropped from the high of ten metres above the present level, which occurred during Aldabra Limestone time, to a staggering 100 metres below. But this was a gradual fall and the rate at which the sea level dropped fluctuated considerably. Evidence of periods early in the fall when the sea level remained more or less constant is preserved on the terraces cut by wave action into the reef-front of the Aldabra Limestone at both eight and four metres above present sea level.

At the peak of the Wurm glacial period, Aldabra must have emerged from the lowered ocean as a precipitous and rocky island of perhaps 400 square kilometres. The limestone cap, probably rimmed and with a shallow central depression, would have been karstic and rugged due to solution weathering, the cavities filling later with calcareous soils. Included in these soils are bone fragments of the terrestrial fauna such as tortoises, crocodiles and birds as well as land snails and crabs.

Sea level steadily rose again as the Wurm glacial period came to an end some 11,000 years ago. Eventually, perhaps 5,000 years ago, the rugged island rim was breached by the rising sea level and the central depression flooded to form the present-day lagoon. Except for local

sand banks adjacent to the channel areas, only fine-grained sediment is thinly accumulating on the relatively flat lagoon floor. Locally on the exposed, terrestrial platform, standing bodies of fresh to brackish water enable stromatolites (algal mounds) to grow. Elsewhere, the platform is vegetated and suffering from weathering and desiccation. Current weathering rates, although dependent on rock type and the degree of exposure, have been estimated at between one millimetre per year along the more sheltered north-west coast to three millimetres per year along the south-east coast with its greater exposure to the elements.

Aldabra Geology in Summary

Coral growth is now limited to the seaward reef slope off Picard, the eroded Malabar shoreline, and in the vicinity of the channels draining the lagoon. Along the coast of Grande Terre a low gravelly storm ridge has formed comprising barchans (parabolic dunes). Guano has only accumulated in certain localities on Picard, but it is sparse and principally occurs in hollows.

The early geology of Aldabra can, on present data, only be speculated on. It seems likely, however, that the seamount foundation had its volcanic birth during the early Miocene about twenty million years ago. Although undoubtedly breaching the sea surface when active, on extinction, subsidence and erosion gradually reduced it to a submarine feature, over perhaps the next ten million years or so. At the same time as at least the latter phases of this destruction, however, was the formation of a surrounding reef. Together these opposing geological forces of substrate subsidence and sediment deposition, along with fluctuating sea levels, slowly created the atoll of today.

The visible geology of the atoll records only the last million years of its history, at most. Yet during that time it is evident that Aldabra has had a start-stop development as a result of the several phases of the Pleistocene ice ages, or glaciations, and the corresponding fluctuations in sea level. Consequently, the geology of Aldabra has at least six cycles of shallow marine carbonate deposition, each separated by weathering surfaces, a terrestrial fauna and, at times, terrestrial sediment accumulation.

During the first five of these marine phases, Aldabra was principally a shallow sub-tidal platform with little coral growth. Only on submergence during the last interglacial period did the ring-shaped raised rim and the depressed central lagoon of a typical atoll develop. But even the formation of the Aldabra Limestone, although more typically coralline, was interrupted by periods of terrestrial emergence as the planet entered the last ice age.

Sea level may have dropped during this last glaciation to as much as 100 metres below the present level. Aldabra was then a high, cliffy island upon which erosion was the dominant active process. While the central depression suffered karstification (weathering by chemical solution), the island's flanks were extensively grooved and channelled by a mechanical weathering process. The slow post-glacial re-submergence of the island to its present level over the past 11,000 years has thus enveloped an atoll that resulted, not from continuous coral growth, but rather from erosion.

Below: Where the champignon rock is heavily dissected,
vegetation takes root in crevices even with tiny
amounts of soil.

Clearly, the fluctuating conditions at Aldabra throughout the late Pleistocene will have influenced both the biological and physical geography of the atoll at any one time. Similar fluctuations are equally likely to have occurred during the earlier glacially-influenced Pleistocene epoch, back to about two million years ago, as well as back through the Pliocene, and possibly into the latest Miocene to perhaps ten million years ago.

With each emergence above sea level Aldabra was colonized by terrestrial flora and fauna that were doomed to extirpation during the ensuing submergence. During their brief sojourn, the many lifeforms were often restricted by geological conditions to specific habitats. For example, pemphis scrub grows today almost exclusively on outcrops of Takamaka Limestone, probably because its component mineral and porosity characteristics are essential to pemphis bushes. The palaeontological sequence of biological flourishings and extinctions at Aldabra thus records the inevitable, though almost imperceptible, control that the planet's geological forces have over its lifeforms.

Aldabra's Geomorphology

The present-day surface morphology of Aldabra is the result of interaction between weathering processes, active since early into the last glacial period some 120,000 years ago,

and the relative resistance of the various exposed rock types. The general topography of the atoll comprises an outer rim, a lagoon, and lagoon channels.

The outer rim is the raised and dissected land ring composed of Aldabra Limestone that rises to a maximum height of only eight metres above sea level and is less than one kilometre wide. To seaward it is flanked by a shallowly dipping (less than five degrees) reef-front slope which begins the plunge to the seamount flanks and oceanic depths. The lagoon is an essentially flat central depression floored principally by Takamaka Limestone with only a thin sediment cover. It is subjected to daily tidal flushings via the lagoon channels which pass through the outer rim, connecting the lagoon with the open ocean. Two main channels and one lesser channel are narrow and deep, all emerging northwards, while a broad complex of shallow channels emerges to the west. All these channels are causing continual erosion on the atoll.

The geomorphological features superimposed upon this typical atoll topography are characteristic of karst terrains and broadly separated into three classes, depending upon the degree of dissection by weathering agents.

Perhaps the most distinctive surface features of the atoll are the mushroom-shaped pinnacles termed, appropriately enough, champignons. They are severely and intricately

dissected and pitted pinnacles of Esprit, Takamaka and Aldabra Limestones with heavily fretted and rasp-like surfaces. On the outer rim these features rise to four metres above sea level, but to only half that height in the lagoon. In some places, the jagged edges have been eroded and smoothed by the action of tortoises clambering over them, but in most areas they are very sharp and rough and present a really difficult terrain to walk on. Champignon arises from present-day weathering by rainfall, often acting upon an already dissected substrate.

Large areas of rough Aldabra Limestone that form the top of the outer rim are termed *pavé*. These more or less flat areas lie eight metres above sea level, and have weathered in places to a depth of half a metre. Large areas of flat Takamaka Limestone adjacent to the lagoon, on the other hand, are termed *platin*. As with the higher *pavé*, they have weathered to a depth of half a metre.

Each of these geomorphological features has developed in response to several factors, such as the original composition of the exposed limestone, its degree of hardness, and the presence of any previous erosion patterns. Their arrangement gives Aldabra its distinctive appearance and, together with the present monsoonal climate, strongly influence the distribution of the terrestrial flora and fauna of today.

3

ALDABRA THE GREEN

KATY BEAVER & LINDSAY CHONG SENG

'How did all these plants reach here? Some seeds certainly arrived by air, stuck to beaks, feet or feathers of birds. Some may even have travelled within a bird's stomach and have been squirted ashore with its droppings. Smaller seeds may have been driven across from the mainland in a storm, supported by their own tiny parachutes of down. Many of the rest will have come by sea. Walk along the beach at high-water mark and you can pick up, within a few yards, half a dozen different kinds of seeds that have been dumped there by the waves. Some may be dead, but many will still be viable and a few may already be sprouting roots and leaves.'
THE LIVING PLANET
David Attenborough

Above: The Aldabra Lily, Lomatophyllum aldabraense, *is the most outstanding of the endemic plants.*

T HE VEGETATION OF ALDABRA IS immensely varied and unusually rich in species for an isolated atoll. Although only three major plant communities form the bulk of the vegetation cover — mangrove, pemphis scrub and mixed scrub — these are not as dull as they sound. Mixed scrub, in particular, is extremely heterogeneous and mangrove areas seen at low tide reveal a hidden world which is often unfamiliar to the visitor (although it may escape attention if the frigatebirds and boobies are nesting in the mangrove branches!) Other smaller plant communities, such as those associated with freshwater pools and those along the outer coastline, add to the diversity, particularly on Picard and at the eastern end of Grande Terre.

Normally, small isolated oceanic islands have a very limited flora, especially if they are flat, because there is not a great range of habitats for plants to occupy. The reason why Aldabra is different in this respect is partly because it is a raised atoll with its land surface some four to eight metres above sea level and partly because it is very large in comparison with most atolls. These features allow the development of inland habitats which are relatively free from the direct influence of the sea. In addition, the varied geological structure of the atoll — champignon, *platin* and *pavé*, with freshwater pools — allows for an increased variety of habitats which can be utilized by plants. Consequently, over thousands of years, species have developed which are adapted to the particular conditions present on Aldabra, species which are different from those on other islands.

Of approximately 176 species of flowering plants which are native to Aldabra, around forty (about twenty-two per cent) are endemic either to Aldabra alone or to Aldabra and a few other nearby raised islands. By comparison, Bird Island, which is a typical small, low, coral sand island on the edge of the granitic Seychelles, has about thirty native flowering plants with no endemic species at all. In contrast, Mahé, which is a high granitic island of much more ancient origin but of similar land area to Aldabra, has some 175 native flowering plant species, of which thirty per cent are endemic.

Another interesting comparison can be made between these three islands. Over forty species of plants have been introduced to Aldabra and a similar number to Bird Island during the course of human settlement (not all have survived, especially on Aldabra). It may sound a lot, but on Mahé something like 600 species have been introduced. They include food plants, spice plants, utility plants (such as sisal and cotton), forest trees and ornamental plants, as well as weeds.

Vegetation growth depends very much on the amount of rainfall, and Aldabra has rather variable annual rainfall as well as a very marked dry season. Only plants which are able to withstand prolonged periods of relative drought are able to survive and the vegetation in some areas becomes bare of leaves or dry and brown towards the end of the dry season. Then, when the rains begin there is a flush of growth and many species flower at this time. This, in turn, affects the activities of insects, birds and tortoises, for example, leading to intense breeding activity between December and March.

Salinity is also a major influence on the vegetation of Aldabra's coastline, so let us look

first at one of the saltiest of habitats, the edges of the lagoon. Here are large expanses of mud and sand and about ninety per cent of the lagoon is fringed with mangrove. It forms a broad ribbon of vegetation as much as one-and-a-half kilometres wide and ten metres high in some places — a thick dark evergreen forest with a maze of winding waterways, where it is easy to lose your sense of direction.

As the mangrove trees live in an intertidal area, their bases are alternately covered and uncovered by the tide twice a day. When the tide falls, their fascinating aerial root systems are revealed — a labyrinth of beautiful arching prop roots and tall knobbly cones, or 'elbows' and 'knees' sticking up out of the mud, or lines of small roots springing up from the sand like rows of upright pencils. All these strange root formations are adaptations which provide the mangrove trees with oxygen and anchorage in the waterlogged, anaerobic and shifting substrate in which they live. Another curious adaptation is adopted by three related mangrove species (*Rhizophora*, *Bruguiera* and *Ceriops*). If you see long green 'fingers' hanging down from between the leaves, you are looking not at a fruit but at the elongated seedling which is growing out of the fruit while it is still attached to the tree. When the seedling eventually drops into the water or mud below the tree, roots grow from the lower tip of the 'finger', anchoring it to the soil and leaves grow out from the opposite

end which is above water. In many countries of the tropical world mangroves are particularly extensive around estuaries because, although they tolerate salt water, they still need fresh water to survive. On Aldabra there are no rivers, so the mangrove trees depend on the rainwater which percolates down through the limestone rock and forms a freshwater 'lens' floating on top of the denser seawater beneath the atoll.

The mangrove forms a plant community which is extremely important for many marine organisms as well as certain birds. Indeed, on Aldabra the mangrove is best known for its role as a major nesting site for colonies of two species of frigatebird and the red-footed booby. But it also forms a vital link between the land and the sea. Many invertebrates live in the mud around the mangrove roots, most of them feeding on the detritus of fallen leaves, fruits, seaweeds, and so on, trapped there. Wading birds such as the crab plover, whimbrel and sandpiper feed on these invertebrates and use the sheltered mangroves as a resting place while on migration, sometimes even overwintering there. Also, the Aldabra rail feeds extensively on the invertebrate fauna of the mangrove swamps. Ecologically, the mangroves form an important breeding ground for many fish, the juveniles of which find an abundance of food and shelter between the submerged roots of the trees. The mangrove habitat as a whole contributes considerably to the turnover of nutrients in the lagoon, enhancing the

growth of coral reef and seagrass beds, both inside the lagoon and on the outer edges of the atoll.

On the landward side of the mangrove there is usually pemphis scrub. *Pemphis acidula* (*bwa-d-anmann*) is a much-branched evergreen shrub which is usually less than two metres high in coastal areas, but farther inland it can grow up to five metres. It is found almost everywhere on Aldabra, either alone or mixed with other scrub vegetation or with the tall *Acrostichum* fern (*fouzer lanmar*). The success of pemphis lies in its ability to grow in the highly dissected champignon rock, often with very little soil, and in its tolerance of salinity, both in salt spray and in the underground water. It has small oval leathery leaves which are covered with a layer of tiny hairs, giving the leaves a grey-green colour and helping to reduce water loss. The small but pretty flowers have six white or creamy petals. Large areas of champignon on Aldabra are covered with almost pure stands of pemphis. Such vegetation is difficult to penetrate because of the dense and tangled growth of the pemphis. Exploration is made more hazardous by the tortuously eroded terrain bristling with sharp points and jagged edges, and pock-marked with pits and small caverns. For the fanciful it could be likened to walking on three-dimensional stone lace that has been woven by an enormous ogre who, wishing to keep his castle secret, has also sewn onto the stone lace a giant pot scourer. For this reason much of the western end of Grande Terre remains virtually unexplored, and our knowledge of the vegetation there comes mainly from aerial photographs. But small areas of pure pemphis scrub which have been investigated reveal fewer species of insects, birds, and other animals, as one would expect in a monoculture.

The vegetation containing the maximum variety of both plant and animal species is the mixed scrub. This is a widespread and variable community, and the particular species present depend on the type of limestone, amount of soil, availability of water, and proximity to the sea. In coastal areas and on champignon, pemphis is common, along with *Scaevola* (*vouloutye*); also *Acalypha claxyloides,* which is an endemic species common in the coastal scrub behind the Research Station, and *Sideroxylon inerme* (*bwa zak*), another endemic which is also common inland. In such locations, mostly on champignon, the mixed scrub is described as 'closed', having a more or less continuous canopy of tall shrubs and small trees. Farther inland, other species become common, for example *Ochna ciliata* (*bwa bouke*), which produces sprays of perfumed yellow flowers; *Apodytes dimidiata* (*bwa none*) whose ripe fruits have a reddish swelling that attracts birds to eat them; *Erythroxylon acranthum* (*sandol*) an endemic species; *Canthium bibracteatum* (*bwa dir*), which is also found on the granitic islands and has orange or red mid-ribs in the leaves; the thorny *Maytenus senegalensis* and *Mystroxylon aethiopicum* (*bwa mozet*). Mixed scrub is extensive in the south-east of Aldabra, on the *platin* limestone and less eroded champignon, where it takes the form of 'open' mixed scrub with scattered small shrubs and areas of tortoise turf, and bare rock or pitted rock containing tiny pockets of soil in which nestle small plants adapted to this situation and often with pretty coloured flowers. Open mixed scrub produces scenery which is typical of the parts of Aldabra frequented by both humans and tortoises. In the

south-east it is sometimes interspersed with groups of taller shrubs and trees called 'groves', of which Takamaka Grove is probably the largest and best known. The groves provide a shaded, sheltered, and humid situation for a number of rare species. Examples are *Carissa edulis* (*bwa sandal*), *Cassipourea thomassetii* (an endemic), *Eugenia elliptica* (an endemic subspecies), *Maillardia pendula* (an endemic) and *Psychotria pervillei* (*bwa koulev*). It seems likely that the presence of these species is evidence of a previously wetter climate on Aldabra, for they are not found outside the groves. Of the species listed, *Eugenia* and *bwa koulev* are very susceptible to attack by coccids (an insect 'pest') and it is possible that these species and also *Maillardia* may already be extinct. Most of the other mixed scrub species are adapted to the semi-drought conditions of the Aldabra dry season. Many have thick leathery leaves and long root systems which reach down to the underground freshwater lens. Deciduous trees and shrubs lose their leaves at this time to prevent excessive loss of water by transpiration. Smaller plants often dry up and die back, relying on bulbs, tubers, or seeds to take them through the dry season.

Every now and then among the mixed scrub that grows in the the flatter parts of the atoll you come across beautiful mown 'lawns'. They are not mown by lawnmowers, of course, but by tortoises. Areas of grassland are much loved by tortoises and are extremely important for them. One type is found along the south-east coast of Grande Terre, on the raised flat land formed by old beaches. This coastal grassland is made up of two grass species, *Sporobolus virginicus* and *Sclerodactylon macrostachyum*, both of which tolerate salt. *Sporobolus* is also found on the coastlines of many coral islands and the granitic islands of Seychelles. It is a spreading grass which can grow up to twenty centimetres tall but when grazed by the tortoises it is only one or two centimetres high. *Sclerodactylon* forms spiky tussocks which are also grazed by the tortoises but not down to lawn level. Many tortoises migrate to the coast at the end of the dry season to feed on the *Sporobolus* when it grows quickly after the first rains. The other type of 'lawn' is called tortoise turf. It is patchy in its distribution, although more widely distributed, and is mainly found on the *platin* and *pavé* at the east end of Grande Terre, in amongst the open mixed scrub, but there is some on Picard also. Tortoise turf consists of a mixture of up to twenty-two species of grasses, sedges, and herbs, the species composition varying somewhat from place to place. Again it is mainly grazed during the rainy season when there is active growth, and much of it becomes brown and dry during the dry season. The attraction of tortoise turf to a tortoise is probably its excellent nutritive value. The fascination of tortoise turf to a botanist, however, is the fact that eight out of the twenty-two species are endemic to Aldabra and twelve are 'genetically dwarfed', that is, they always remain small plants even when freed from grazing. This suggests that the tortoise turf community has evolved on Aldabra under constant grazing pressure from tortoises, and some species have adapted to this situation by becoming dwarfed, thereby enabling them to flower and produce seeds even when tiny.

In the south-east of Grande Terre, where there are freshwater pools and land which is flooded during the rainy season, a number of smaller plant communities exist. The most

Top: the beautiful yellow flowers of Thespesia populneoides
live for just one day, gradually darkening to deep orange
as the day progresses. Centre left: Tournefortia, *another salt-resistant*
bush. Bottom left: the endemic subspecies of the tropicbird orchid
Angraecum eburneum *grows on some of the small islets in*
West Channels. Centre right: Capparis cartilaginea *is a low*
prickly bush whose flower is a mass of long white
stamens, which open at night and fall to the ground during the
*following day. Bottom right:*Tribulus cistoides *fruits*
are prickly, making it uncomfortable to walk on.

obvious includes the screwpine (*vakwa*) *Pandanus tectorius* with its long stiff sword-like leaves and basal cone of stilt roots, and *Thespesia populneoides* (*bwa-d-roz*) a small tree with large yellow flowers. Also present is *Lumnitzera racemosa* (*mangliye pti fey*), a mangrove species normally associated with the landward edge of the mangrove where fresh water is more abundant. Freshwater pools are common and extensive during the rainy season but during the dry season most pools dry up. Spreading out over the mud of such pools are two small plants — *Mollugo oppositifolia* and *Bacopa monnieri* — which form a carpet that suddenly becomes very striking when the *Bacopa* produces a mass of tiny white or pale pinkish-blue flowers. There is only one aquatic flowering plant on Aldabra, *Najas*, which is a delicate and much-branched plant with thread-like leaves, found in some of the more permanent pools. However, a common phenomenon is the presence of large masses, or flocs, of algae floating on the water surface. One of the fascinating features of many freshwater pools is their rise and fall according to the level of the tide in the lagoon and outside the atoll. This happens because the fresh water lies on top of sea water and an underground network of channels in the limestone directly links the pools to the sea. One day you visit a pool it may be very shallow, and the next week you visit it again and it has risen, even though there has been no rainfall.

There are other communities present on the coast of Aldabra. Most conspicuous are the groups of tall *(Casuarina equisetifolia)* trees and coconut palms which stick up prominently above all the other vegetation. In fact, when you are crossing the huge lagoon in a small boat, groves of casuarina may be the only bits of 'land' you can see shimmering on the horizon. Coconuts have probably arrived on the atoll by natural means, although they were also planted deliberately during settlement times. It is uncertain whether casuarina was purposely introduced or not, but it certainly spread with human assistance, although the groves now continue to expand naturally. Casuarina is an evergreen tree of Australian origin which looks like a conifer, though its long thin 'needles' have a very different structure. Few plants can grow beneath casuarina trees because of the thick carpet of needles, the presence of which seems to affect the chemistry of the soil and may even directly inhibit the growth of other species. Other coastal species, such as *Guettarda*, *Tournefortia*, *Ipomoea pes-caprae*, and *Thespesia populnea*, which are also typical of low coral islands and the beach fronts of the granitic islands, are present on Aldabra, but there are relatively few beaches since the atoll's rim is mostly rugged champignon limestone. The sand dunes of the south-east coast present an interesting habitat not found on low coral islands or the granitic islands. They are inhabited by bushes such as *Suriana*, *Tournefortia*,

and *Scaevola,* as well as grasses such as *Lepturus* and *Sporobolus.* During the period of the south-east trade winds, the intensity of the wind is such that trees and bushes become extremely distorted. *Guettarda* trees in particular grow almost horizontally because the wind brings in salt spray from the enormous waves (which also deposit on land an amazing variety of marine junk such as plastic shoes and toys, fishing floats and polystyrene blocks).

The coastal species occur throughout the tropical region and are brought to Aldabra by ocean currents. How did other plants arrive and where did they come from? A relatively large proportion of species are derived from East Africa, Madagascar, the Mascarenes and the granitic Seychelles. It seems likely that animals have been important in the colonization process, particularly birds and tortoises. Fruit-eaters such as pigeons and bulbuls could have brought species such as *Ficus, Ochna* and *Sideroxylon.* Other birds may have brought sticky seeds on their feet or plumage, for example *Bacopa* and *Plumbago aphylla* (*lerb payanke*). Tortoises were also important as they eat a great variety of herbs, grasses, sedges and shrubs, including fruits. Food passes through their gut extremely slowly and, because some seeds will pass right through the tortoise's digestive tract and emerge still alive and ready to germinate, tortoises arriving on Aldabra after one or two weeks floating in the sea from Madagascar could easily have introduced new species. Over the thousands of years since

Aldabra last emerged as an atoll, evolution in the harsh and isolated conditions, probably under an unstable climate, resulted in the development of a relatively large number of unique species. The presence of 'relict' species which survive only in the shelter of the groves or thickets mentioned earlier provides evidence that these evolutionary processes are continuing.

Of the endemic flowering plants, the best known and most spectacular is the Aldabra lily, *Lomatophyllum aldabraense*, which has a circle of long fleshy pointed leaves, sometimes at the end of a thick stem. It is more common in the west and north of the atoll, where it flowers mainly towards the end of the rainy season and produces a conspicuous spike of tubular orange-red flowers, followed by round berries which turn purple-red. There is an endemic subspecies of the tropicbird orchid, *Angraecum eburneum,* which has sprays of beautiful white flowers. It is found on some of the small islets. *Pandanus aldabraensis* is an endemic screwpine species which is only found in a few areas (Takamaka and near Johnny Channel). Two endemic species of *Grewia* occur, one with yellow flowers, the other with pink flowers and large hairy fruits. The other endemics are not very impressive to non-botanists, but include common shrubs such as *Sideroxylon* and *Acalypha*, and smaller plants such as some of the tortoise turf species. However, there are quite a number of interesting indigenous plants on Aldabra which also occur in countries such as Madagascar. *Capparis cartilaginea* (*bwa zanget*) is a low prickly bush whose flower is a mass of long white stamens. It opens at night and the stamens fall to the ground during the following day. Fairly common on Picard, it flowers mainly in the dry season. Also flowering during the dry season is the orchid *Acampe rigida*, which has red-splotched yellow flowers. It is found on Picard and some of the smaller islets. *Ochna* (*bwa bouke*) has already been mentioned, with its yellow flowers usually produced at the end of the dry season when it is still without leaves. A species of jasmine, *Jasminum elegans*, occurs with beautifully scented white flowers. *Azima tetracantha* is a shrub with four long spines at each node. It is much liked by tortoises in spite of the spines.

Mention should also be made of the non-flowering plants, which are often overlooked. The number of species is low compared with the granitic islands because of the relatively arid conditions. Apart from two ferns, one of which is large and quite common (*Acrostichum*, which tolerates salinity), there are several moss species and a number of lichens and fungi, although the latter two groups have scarcely been studied. A common moss species on tree trunks is *Calymperes tenerum* which can reproduce asexually and is, therefore, not as dependent on water as most other mosses.

More than forty plant species have been introduced to Aldabra by man. About half were brought purposely as sources of food and other commodities, for example vegetables, papaya, cotton and sisal. Some were probably brought in accidentally and are typical weed species such as *Lantana camara* (*vyeyfiy*) and *Stachytarpheta jamaicensis* (*zepi ble*). However, a few of the introduced weeds may actually have been brought in purposely as medicinal plants, for example: *Turnera ulmifolia* (*koket*), *Catharanthus roseus* (Madagascar periwinkle or

roz anmer), *Eleusine indica* (*pat-d-poul*), *Datura metel* (*fler pwazon*), *Vernonia cinerea* (*gerivit*) and *Sida rhombifolia* (*lerb dir*). Some of these plants have remained confined to areas near habitation and coconut plantations. Others have naturalized and have spread further afield — notable examples are *Stachytarpheta*, sisal, and *Passiflora suberosa* (*lepeka*). Most of them have been aided in their dispersal by birds and tortoises. These particular introduced species are very successful plants and they may become as dominant in some locations on Aldabra as they have done on other tropical islands.

Ecosystems exist in some sort of balance or equilibrium but the equilibrium is a dynamic one and may change over time. Over hundreds of years various factors alter — the sea level may rise or fall, the climate may become hotter and drier, new plant and animal species may arrive. Such events have occurred on Aldabra and are still occurring. Other changes are brought about by humans and this is when the balance is sometimes severely tested. The capture of large numbers of tortoises in the nineteenth century caused changes in the vegetation on Aldabra. Later, when the tortoise population was allowed to build up again, there appeared to be large-scale destruction of vegetation in heavily populated areas. There are signs that the tortoise population is in the process of naturally regulating itself (by laying fewer eggs, for example; see Chapter Five) so that some kind of balance should be restored eventually. Tortoises certainly do affect the vegetation, not only directly by feeding on grass and tortoise turf, but also by eating young seedlings, so reducing natural regeneration. On the other hand, by eating fruits, tortoises are helping to disperse the seeds of many plants. Their faeces are also an important food source for smaller animals and eventually the breakdown products enrich the soil. However, when tortoises seek shade during the hot part of the day, they trample undergrowth and disturb the soil and roots beneath bushes. These activities may eventually result in the death of shade bushes.

For a time it was thought that feral goats were not having a particularly destructive effect on the Aldabra vegetation. However, populations in some areas multiplied to such an extent that damage became more obvious. Goats are mainly browsers, feeding on leaves and shoots of shrubs and trees and are notorious for producing substantial changes in vegetation. They break branches while trying to reach fresh growth and also eat seedlings. A smaller animal which has had a devastating effect on some plant species is an insect. The coccid or mealy bug, *Icerya seychellarum*, may have been accidentally introduced to Aldabra in the 1960s and by the 1970s had become a major pest. It is a small insect, covered with a mass of white fluffy wax, that sucks the sap of many plant species. Some trees and bushes are heavily infested and the underside of the leaves support large numbers of coccids clustered around the veins. Goats and these coccids are not native to Aldabra and the vegetation is not adapted to their presence. Stress is as much a health problem for plants as it is for humans. Browsing by goats and removal of sap by coccids are additional stresses for plants which are already stressed by lack of water during the dry season, together with strong winds and salt spray. People who have been visiting Aldabra over many years have noted the death of large numbers of trees in the south-east of the atoll, where shade is very limited for tortoises. Both goats and coccids threaten the survival of the tortoises in that area and also important parts of the Aldabra vegetation itself, so measures have had to be taken to reduce their numbers.

Human settlement of an island may portend the introduction of alien species, but it also heralds a knowledge of the organisms that live there, often previously unknown. It is surprising how many of the native Aldabra plants have acquired vernacular names. Plants are given names because they possess certain characteristics — they may be similar to already familiar plants, or have distinctive fruits or flowers or, more importantly, discovered to have some special use. On Aldabra, older workers will tell you that a certain plant is good for driving away mosquitoes, another makes excellent *moutya* drums, another has hard straight stems for poles, another is good for stomach complaints, and so on. Aldabra seems to have acquired a reputation in Seychelles folklore as a vast treasure house of medicinal plants. Why? Is it something to do with Aldabra's remoteness or the unfamiliarity of many of the plants? Many that are used are endemic, such as *sandol* (*Erythroxylon acranthum*) and *bwa trwa fey* (*Malleastrum leroyi*). Others are parasitic on other plants, which may have significance in the eyes of herbalists, such as *bwa mamay* (*Viscum triflorum*) and *mangoula* (*Bakerella clavata*). Unfortunately for the plants, although some are

very common (for example *bwa zak, Sideroxylon*) and can withstand constant collection, others are rare (for example *mangoula*) and collection may have already led to their extinction. Many Seychellois know the story of the plant on Aldabra whose leaves do not move at all even though it is a terribly windy day and yet on a still day the leaves tremble and shake...does that tree still exist? The Seychellois would have you believe so.

It must be said that we humans are good at creating problems for our environment — often innocently, often by accident, often for the best of reasons (at least at the time), but nevertheless with often fateful consequences. Thank goodness so much natural vegetation and such diversity survives on Aldabra, in spite of the problems.

4

THE LIVING LABORATORY

RON GERLACH & DR JUSTIN GERLACH

'Aldabra is one of nature's last ditches.'
NEW STATESMAN
Nigel Calder

Above: The striking black-and-white beetle, Mausoleopsis
aldabraensis, *is an important pollinator for many plants.*

IT HAS LONG BEEN REALIZED THAT isolated island groups and remote islands represent a microcosm of evolution. The remoteness and harsh, inhospitable nature of Aldabra means that the course of evolution has been less disrupted by man than in most other areas. This provides scientists and those interested in ecology and the natural environment with a treasure house of information.

Geologists have established that Aldabra has been submerged below the sea several times in its history, most recently about 125,000 years ago. The remains of the fauna that existed on the atoll in between inundations have been preserved as fossil shells and bones in holes in the limestone providing a record of the processes of colonization and evolution that have occurred in the past.

Colonization and establishment of populations of new species have taken place over the years since the re-emergence of Aldabra. The vast expanse of sea makes colonization of such a remote island an extremely haphazard occurrence. The means by which species find their way to the atoll depend upon the type of organism concerned. Flying animals (birds, bats and insects) are able to colonize without assistance, larger flightless forms (such as reptiles) are most likely to cross the sea by 'rafting' (drifting on pieces of floating vegetation in the sea currents). Lighter organisms can be carried accidentally on the feet of birds or blown across the sea by strong winds. Plants may reach the island by rafting, accidental transport, wind dispersal, or by floating on the sea. Modern methods of transport by boat and by man's wishing to brighten up his life, are usually regarded as 'introductions' but these could be seen as equally valid means for organisms to extend their range.

Colonization is only the first stage in the establishment of plants and animals in a new environment. Plants may find themselves in an environment without a pollinator, animals may not find sufficient familiar food sources. With the small numbers of colonists, finding mates may also be a problem. In all cases it becomes a matter of 'adapt or die' and it is this adaptation to a new environment that forms the basis for evolution.

Colonization of Aldabra seems to have taken place mainly from the Malagasy region via the Comoros Islands. Many of the atoll's species have Malagasy affinities but the second sphere of influence is from the nearby African continent. Strong steady wind cycles from south-east (from Madagascar) and west and north-west (from Africa) would assist both rafting and wind-blown colonization. Large rafts of bamboo have been recorded along the coast of the atoll during the south-east trade winds, these are probably of Malagasy origin. It has been calculated that with the aid of the steady surface currents and wind, the 420 kilometres from Madagascar could be covered in three to nine days.

With the exception of winged species, only one animal has colonized Aldabra by its own power, without rafting or being wind-blown. This is the crocodile; found only as fossil remains, having failed to recolonize since the last submergence of the atoll. This species was originally identified as the Nile crocodile, *Crocodylus niloticus*, but, like the Seychelles population that was killed off in the 1800s, they were probably estuarine crocodiles, *Crocodylus porosus*. The estuarine crocodile is the only regularly sea-faring species and has

been encountered 1,000 kilometres from land, in the western Pacific, making it a very able colonist. On Aldabra, fossil remains date from two periods separated by submersion events, demonstrating that colonization from its normal east-Asian range occurred at least twice. The large ocean-going estuarine crocodiles were abundant around the central islands of Seychelles when the islands were first explored in the 1700s. When they were present on Aldabra their influence on the coastal environment must have been considerable. Since their extinction during the last submergence of the atoll, large predatory animals have been absent from the land.

Another reptile species found only as fossils is the iguana, *Oplurus cuvieri*, a species that still survives on Madagascar and the Comoros. The iguana fossilized on Aldabra seems to have been over sixty centimetres long, making it larger than the living form. It may have been a uniquely Aldabran race or species but the fossils are too fragmentary to be sure. Other fossil reptiles included the geckos, *Paroedura sp.* and *Geckolepis maculata*, and the skinks, *Scelotes sp.* and *Mabuya maculilabris*; all of these species seem to be most closely related to Malagasy forms.

Present-day reptiles, excluding the tortoises (See Chapter 5), consist of only four species; three geckos and one skink. The Pacific gecko (*Gehyra mutilata*) is a recent introduction and

is the most common species associated with man throughout the Indo-Pacific region. However, it is not certain if the Pacific gecko has succeeded in establishing itself on Aldabra. On Mahé, Praslin and La Digue this is the common lizard seen at night inside buildings, usually around lights which attract the flying insects upon which they feed. Pacific geckos can change colour with their temperament or to resemble their background, from brownish when on tree trunks, to pinkish near bright lights. They can shed their tails or skin when attacked by predators, enabling them to escape. By day they hide in crevices among rocks or in buildings behind pictures. The genus *Gehyra* contains about twenty-one species, of which the Pacific gecko is the only one to have invaded the Indian Ocean from the Pacific. Almost certainly introduced by man, it could have reached Aldabra by a circuitous route through Madagascar or Mauritius to the granitic islands and thence to Aldabra. In Seychelles it is known as *lezar disik*, meaning sugar lizard, due to its supposed sweet tooth.

They are able to walk or even run across ceilings and up window panes as their feet are equipped with closely ranged *lamellae* (ridges) which act almost like small strips of velcro. Their small round eggs are usually laid on protected ledges or inside rolled up blinds, numbering two or three and lightly fused together. They hatch in about sixty days. The habit of living in houses and laying eggs on ledges or in crevices means that they are especially well adapted to being dispersed by human activity.

The other nocturnal gecko is the wandering house gecko (*Hemidactylus mercatorius*). Unlike the Pacific gecko, it forages under leaves and on trees (though not exclusively). It is easily distinguished from the patternless Pacific gecko by the strong, dark, waved bands traversing the body, and the skin is more heavily textured with small tubercles on the back. The colour varies, resembling the background to some degree and changing with mood. Females lay two spherical eggs at almost any time of the year. Though common in houses, they also thrive on uninhabited islands and forage on the ground. They are found in the Aldabra group, Farquhar group, and Coetivy but not the Amirantes or granitic Seychelles. On Cosmoledo they live in association with red-footed boobies, where they feed on insects attracted by discarded food and droppings.

The Abbott's day gecko (*Phelsuma abbotti abbotti*) is a northern Madagascan species. They are slender, the back dull greyish-green, unlike the brilliant green phelsuma of the granitic Seychelles. The belly is white and the legs and flanks are boldly mottled black and white. On Assumption, the closely related *Phelsuma abbotti sumptio* is larger, stockier, with a more bluish back and yellow belly. The races of Abbott's day gecko on Aldabra and Assumption each show an early stage of divergent evolution from the Malagasy parent. Each race resembles the parent form more closely than it does its neighbouring island relative. Probably, Assumption and Aldabra were independently colonized by this species from Madagascar. Fossil records show that phelsuma have colonized Aldabra several times.

The highest densities of Abbott's day gecko occur in coconut palms on Aldabra, although they appear to feed on the nectar of coconut flowers less than on other islands. They are often seen in association with tortoises, especially during the period after the north-west

monsoon (around March), when the tortoise growth rates increase in response to improved food availability. This increased growth results in softening of the sutures between the scutes on the tortoises, the soft skin is attacked by mosquitoes and flies upon which phelsuma feed. They have been known to ride on the carapace for some days taking insects that are attracted to the tortoise, even hiding under the carapace at night, or when alarmed.

Bouton's snake-eyed skink (*Cryptoblepharus boutonii*) is sometimes referred to as the fishing skink because it preys on small crustaceans and fish along the littoral. This island specialist is widely distributed but has two main population centres: one in the Indo-Australo-Pacific and the second in the East Africa-western Indian Ocean region. Aldabran skinks appear, not surprisingly, to be more closely related to the latter group. As this is the only ground-dwelling lizard species to be seen on Aldabra, the lack of competition has resulted in their being widespread in all habitats and not confined to coastal areas, thus occupying a much wider ecological niche than elsewhere. It is, however, along the intertidal zone that they demonstrate their unusual adaptation to this habitat. Not only are they adept at catching small fish, but they are also able to withstand salt water and will take refuge in tidal pools to escape a predator. On Madagascar they are known to eat young mudskippers. This tolerance of sea-water and the habit of foraging below the high tide line help explain

why Bouton's skink has colonized so many islands successfully. The soft-shelled eggs number only one or two and are laid in the moist sand above the high tide mark.

Bouton's snake-eyed skink and Abbott's day gecko, being diurnal, are the main food source for the diminutive Malagasy kestrel. They are also preyed upon by coucals, drongos, herons, crows and rails.

The high energy requirements of mammals means that they are less able to tolerate periods of enforced starvation than reptiles. This makes them poor natural colonists. Other than the introduced goats, cats and rats, the only mammals to be found are bats. The largest species is the Aldabran fruit bat (*Pteropus seychellensis aldabraensis*). This large fruit-eating species is a subspecies of the Seychelles fruit bat. The Aldabran subspecies also occurs on the Comoros. As the largest fruit-eating animals on most small Indian Ocean islands, fruit bats are important agents of dispersal for all fruit-producing trees and thus of importance in tropical island ecosystems. Aldabran fruit bats have been seen eating the fruits of takamaka (*Calophyllum inophyllum*), Indian almond (*Terminalia catappa*), *Mystroxylon aethiopicum*, and the three ficus species (*Ficus avi-avi, F. nautarum,* and *F. reflexa*), together with sisal flowers. Aldabran fruit bats have been seen mating throughout the year, although most young are born in November and December.

Below: A hermit crab scavenges for food close to Cinq Cases.

Below: A hermit crab scavenges for food close to Cinq Cases.

The other bat species on Aldabra are small insectivores of African or Madagascan origin. Three species have been recorded: the Mauritian bat (*Taphozous mauritianus*), the Aldabran free-tailed bat (*Tadarida pumila*), and Touessart's trident bat (*Triaenops furculus*). All three are nocturnal and roost by day in hollow trees, in small groups or singly.

Land crabs are the largest of the atoll's invertebrates and occupy most habitats. They are the most important scavengers and detritivores and are, therefore, essential to the energy cycle. There are twenty-four species in all, ranging from those confined to the shoreline to the terrestrial species such as the coconut or robber crab (*Birgus latro*) and the terrestrial hermit crabs (*Coenobita perlata, C. brevimana, C. cavipes,* and *C. rugosa*). Their presence on Aldabra is as a result of their larvae being transported to the atoll on sea currents; all crabs deposit their eggs in the sea, the larvae spend many months developing in the plankton before emerging onto land. This life cycle leads to all species being very widespread, and this is one of the few animal groups on Aldabra that does not include endemic species or races.

The very abundant species; robber crabs, cardisoma crabs, and terrestrial hermit crabs, are all known to be herbivorous and are thus essential in the breakdown of vegetation, fallen leaves, and other organic detritus. All these terrestrial species are known to feed on tortoise

faeces. *Coenobita*, in particular, occupy the shaded rest areas used by the tortoises and will often burrow into the soil, taking the faeces directly into the soil. Crab burrows aid the aeration and drainage of the soil, although the porous nature of the ground does not seem to need this sort of assistance.

Robber crabs are the largest terrestrial arthropods on Aldabra, and possibly the largest in the world. A large male specimen can measure up to one metre from leg tip to leg tip. Robber crabs are members of the hermit crab group, and juveniles find protection by living in sea shells in the early, vulnerable, part of their existence. When they outgrow the available shells, they may sometimes take up home in a half coconut shell, but will eventually resort to digging burrows like the adults. Burrows also help them prevent desiccation by avoiding the tropical sun in the day, to emerge to feed at night. The use of burrows also eliminates the need to find and carry increasingly larger shells and removes restrictions on growth. Increased size means increased power: other species of crabs and even rats have been seen to abandon food when a robber crab approaches. These animals seldom return until the robber crab has finished, and if they do, they are swiftly deterred by the crab lifting one or both of its front legs in a threatening manner which is clearly understood by the intruder. Unlike other crabs, robber crabs prefer to eat alone and their

*Opposite: The powerful pincers of the robber crab enable them
to tear apart rotting coconuts by breaking open the top of the shell
and gouging out the flesh.*

*Below: The robber crab, common on Aldabra, is possibly the world's largest
terrestrial arthropod.*

size deters competitors. Coconuts are not their only source of food and most inhabit areas where the vegetation is dominated by other plants. On Grande Terre, the largest population inhabits the pandanus thickets. They generally feed on rotting coconuts by breaking the top of the shell and gouging out the meat with their pincers. Other food includes fruits, rotting leaves and almost any organic material, even their own moulted exoskeletons. There is also evidence of cannibalism, which can be expected to arise where victims originating from other populations share little genetic similarity with the resident individuals (as with robber crabs) and where new recruits from another population lower the chances of reproductive success of the residents through pressure on limited resources.

As with all crabs, growth makes it necessary to shed the hard outer shell (or exoskeleton) periodically. At this point they retreat into their burrows and seal the entrance with a plug of mud. They remain hidden for a period of about thirty days, living on a deposit of fat built up prior to moulting.

More common and widespread than the robber crab is *Cardisoma carnifex*, which inhabits virtually all the environments above high tide level. The mangrove crab, *Cardisoma rotunda*, tends to be more selective in its choice of habitat and can be found along the tidal edges of mud flats and mangroves. These somewhat intimidating-looking crabs are herbivorous and,

like the robber crabs, are responsible for vegetation recycling. Living in the mud of the mangroves and on the mud flats are the fiddler crabs (*Uca chlorophthalmus, U. tetragonon* and *U. lactea*), so called because of the male's one exaggerated pincer that is moved slowly back and forth in the manner of a fiddler manipulating a bow. The enlarged turquoise or orange pincer is found only in males; females have dull, normal-sized ones. The males use the pincers as signals to attract females or to defend their territories from other males. They are not weapons, only being used as signals or threats in ritualized arm-waving displays. Fiddler crabs, while contributing to the general breakdown of vegetation and dead animals into the mud, are also an essential element in the food chain for many shorebirds (especially crab plovers), herons, and rails. This applies equally to the young of most crustaceans, including the shoreline species such as ghost crabs (*Ocypoda* sp.) and *Geograpsus*. These latter species are in turn predators on turtle hatchlings. Rock crabs (*Grapsus fourmanoiri* and *G. tenuicrustatus*) are extremely fast-moving crabs on littoral rocks. They browse on algae, scraping them off the rocks with specialized pincers. While scraping off the algae, small quantities of the coral limestone rock are scraped off, consumed, and expelled as grit particles that contribute to the production of beach sand.

Terrestrial molluscs are well adapted to colonization by being dispersed by rafting or on

birds' feet, or by being wind-blown in the case of many minute species. As with all other animal groups, most forms on Aldabra are of Madagascan or African origin, good examples being the minute carnivorous *Gulella* snails. One endemic subspecies, *G. gwendolinae aldabrae*, occurs at present, two others are known from fossils, *G. dentiens* and *G. peakei*. The latter was an endemic species closely related to African forms. *G. dentiens* and *G. gwendolinae* are African species. Very little is known of these species as they are less than two millimetres long. They are known to be carnivorous and probably feed on minute insect larvae and nematode worms.

The largest species is *Rachis aldabrae*, a purple and orange-banded arboreal snail up to twenty millimetres long. This genus is found in forest patches throughout central and southern Africa. The terrestrial *Tropidophora gardineri* is half the size of *Rachis*. *Tropidophora* is related to marine snails and retains the operculum that closes the mouth of the shell. This operculum acts as a defence against predators and hostile environments which may result in some immunity to salt water. This makes them excellent candidates for rafting to new areas, or possibly even floating on the surface of the sea. Another operculate species which exists on Aldabra, *Cyathopoma picardense*, is more likely to have been transported by birds; the long hairs on the shell make it likely that this species will occasionally be trapped in mud on birds' feet. *Cyathopoma* is an Asiatic genus, as is *Kaliella*, a typically Indian form.

This species is still to be described scientifically so its precise relationships to other species are not clear. Both these genera occur on several of the granitic islands of Seychelles, which probably represent the most likely sources of colonists.

The smallest terrestrial species is *Gastrocopta tripunctata*, which is less than two-and-a-half millimetres long. This species has tooth-like extensions of the lip of the shell, which form barriers preventing snail-eating insects from entering the mouth of the shell. This is also found in the carnivorous *Gulella* species. With its microscopic size and pan-tropical distribution it is probable that *Gastrocopta* has spread by accidental transport by birds and by wind dispersal as 'aerial plankton'. Snails of the Subulinid group are often viewed as having been introduced. Only one species, *Allopeas javanicum*, is recorded on Aldabra at present. However, species of this genus are very similar in appearance and are extremely difficult to identify; there are probably several species on Aldabra. One Subulinid is known from a fossil on Aldabra, indicating that some species may be natural colonists.

The mud snail *Quickia aldabraensis* is an endemic form of the pan-tropical *Q. concisa*. Forms of this type of snail have colonized Aldabra many times, as witnessed by fossils from all stages of Aldabra's history. Several widespread coastal species also exist. These species (*Assiminea parvula*, *A. punctum*, *Melampus caffra*, *M. lividus* and *Truncatella guerini*) have

marine larvae and can thus easily reach oceanic islands by drifting on the sea currents. One further species is worth mentioning; *Bulimus bavayi* is a freshwater species. As the presence of fresh water on Aldabra is normally a temporary event following rain, the presence of a freshwater species is surprising. Biochemical studies show that the Aldabran population is only very recently descended from Madagascan colonists. The regular drying out of water pools means that the population probably undergoes regular restocking from Madagascar, perhaps carried out by birds accidentally transporting snail eggs.

In this environment of temporary freshwater and brackish pools held in the eroded limestone, with mixed evergreen and deciduous scrub interspersed with the open areas of short grasses, sedges and ephemeral herbs, insects participate in all the essential functions as pollinators, dung eaters, blood suckers, and as a link in the food chain. Without pollinators, the plant life of Aldabra would be limited to a few species capable of reproducing by cloning. Large pollinators, like sunbirds and bats, are able to pollinate only a limited range of plants, and it must fall to the insects to provide the generalist pollinators. A small, but striking black-and-white beetle, *Mausoleopsis aldabraensis*, appears to have evolved to fill this niche. Many other insects are involved in this important function, but none except *Mausoleopsis aldabraensis* is ubiquitous. Many of the Aldabran insects are widespread, active

species, such as the Afro-Malagasy butterflies, damselflies, and dragonflies. The latter groups rely on the temporary pools of fresh water as their larvae are aquatic.

Visitors to the granitic Seychelles often comment on the rarity of butterflies there. By contrast, there are a number of colourful species on Aldabra. Legrand, a correspondent of the Paris Museum of Natural History, who visited Seychelles in 1956 and 1958–1960, recorded about 130 species of Lepidoptera in the Aldabra group, of which fifty or so were endemic. Particularly conspicuous or common are the blue pansy (*Junonia orythya*), eyed pansy (*J. oenone epiclelia*), blue commodore (*J. rhadama*), common African leopard (*Phalanta phalanta aethiopica*), Aldabran white (*Belenois aldabraensis*), Aldabran orange tip (*Colotis evanthides*), Aldabran grass yellow (*Eurema floricola*), broad-bordered grass yellow (*E. brigitta pulchella*), freckled fan (*Acraea ranavalona*), dancing fan (*A. neobule legrandi*), and African monarch (*Danaus chrysippus*).

On the basis of collections made during Royal Society expeditions, the insect species of Aldabra are estimated to be in the region of 1,000. In contrast with the granitic islands, the fauna is derived almost entirely from the Afro-tropical and Malagasy region. Only four per cent of insects are shared between Aldabra and the granitic Seychelles and only one per cent has Oriental affinities. The endemic element, about thirty-eight per cent, is astonishingly

high considering the maximum period that the atoll has been above sea level since its last submergence, which is probably around 125,000 years.

One insect species in particular has received much attention recently. This is the mealy bug, *Icerya seychellarum*. This sap-sucking insect may infest plants in great numbers, possibly leading to damage to the plant. In some countries, infestation has been associated with plant diseases which are probably transmitted by the mealy bugs. Although the females are wingless, mealy bugs are very widely dispersed, certainly through accidental human transportation, but probably also naturally by wind dispersal of tiny juveniles.

With *Icerya seychellarum* having a very long history in Seychelles and a high probability of being native there, colonization of Aldabra may have been a natural event, although there are no records of its occurrence prior to 1968. However, the presence of this known plant pest led to measures being taken to eradicate it by means of biological control, using predatory coccinellid beetles. This does not seem to have had the effects expected. There is a possibility that the increase in mealy bug infestation since the 1960s may be part of an interaction between insect pests (including *Icerya* and leaf-mining moths and flies) and goat browsing. It is difficult to separate cause from effect, but there may be an association between heavy goat browsing and heavy insect infestation, whether one leads to the other or whether both are responding to another factor such as climatic stress on the plant is far from clear.

The majority of the insect species on Aldabra are small, little studied, leaf litter-inhabiting species which coexist with a diverse litter fauna of woodlice, millipedes, centipedes and spiders. These include many species recorded only from Aldabra, although this may not necessarily mean that they are endemic to Aldabra as these groups are very poorly known in the region. The woodlice are represented by thirteen known species, of which six are described as endemics, five are found elsewhere in the western Indian Ocean, one is pantropical, and one probably introduced. Most of the species are found in areas subject to sea spray, salt tolerance is to be expected from organisms that probably colonized by rafting.

The insect life of Aldabra is heavily influenced by both the salt spray and the low rainfall on the atoll. Low rainfall may account for the small numbers of insect species that parasitize plants or animals; these groups are much scarcer on Aldabra than on other islands in the region or on mainland Africa. The strong sea influence results in conditions that are ideal for the Tabanid shore-flies. These small flies are normally restricted to the shoreline, where they feed on and breed in seaweed washed up on the coast. On Aldabra they are found in all habitats and have become the main insect type feeding on decaying plant matter, elsewhere in the world this niche is normally occupied by the Drosophilid fruit flies.

The terrestrial fauna of Aldabra is characterized by such unusual traits of ecology and behaviour. This arises firstly from the isolation of the atoll which results in only a small selection of animal groups colonizing the land. This fauna has several groups missing that normally occupy important niches, and the successful colonists adapt to fill these niches. The strong sea influence further modifies the adaptations of the colonists so that they evolve to fill unfamiliar niches while being constrained by a harsh climate of low rainfall and desiccating salt-spray-laden winds. The result of this is an environment dominated by a large herbivorous reptile (the giant tortoise), seabird colonies, and large numbers of terrestrial crabs, which coexist with a range of equally important, but less obvious, minute molluscs and arthropods.

5

KINGDOM OF THE GIANT TORTOISE

DR MALCOLM COE

'These contemporaries of the dodo have fat round feet like those of elephants, and bronze scales with burnished rings, like the age rings in a cross section of polished wood, and their fossil bones are almost as old as the island of Aldabra.'
BLUE MERIDIAN
Peter Matthiessen

Above: Unlike most tortoises, the giant tortoise of Aldabra has a flat nose enabling it to drink from shallower pools in the coral limestone by drawing in water through its nostrils.

A PPROACHING ALDABRA, THE VISITOR is immediately struck by the narrow band of sand and coral limestone which clears the sea surface by no more than a few metres. In the south-east corner, a small band of limestone reaches nine metres above sea level, but except for a few small (and transient) sand dunes, most of the atoll seems very insecure compared with the huge granitic masses which emerge from the sea in the vicinity of Mahé. The history of Aldabra illustrates this observation well, for although absolute dates are uncertain it is clear that the atoll has been submerged below the sea and subsequently re-emerged during the rise and fall of sea level induced by the major glaciations. Indeed it seems probable that over the last million years the land surface of Aldabra has been submerged as many as six times (see Chapter Two). The consequence of these events would be that living organisms found on the atoll today have been carried there by sea, wind, or animal (including human) agency.

The reptiles, as we see, are no exception to this rule, and on several occasions in the past the justly famous giant land tortoises of Aldabra *Geochelone* (*Dipsochelys*) *gigantea* have floated there from other islands in the Indian Ocean. Such a mode of marine transport may seem unusual, or even impossible, but the frequency of giant tortoises living on the islands of the Indian Ocean, the Caribbean, the Pacific and the Mediterranean indicates just how common such a mode of transport must have been.

Chelonia, the group comprising turtles and tortoises, evolved about 180 million years ago. They came to dominate many environments, to be later replaced by large carnivorous mammals. Aldabra remains a living museum, dominated by an ancient race of large, herbivorous reptiles — the giant tortoises. Sadly these large, inoffensive, slow-moving creatures were no match for human beings, who have been responsible for the extinction of all the island populations in the world, except those of Aldabra and the Galapagos Islands, off the coast of Ecuador. Extinctions in the granitic Seychelles included Marion's tortoise (*Dipsochelys holoissa*) and possibly other unique species which had survived for perhaps millions of years prior to the arrival of man. However, it is not certain whether the minor differences of the granitic Seychelles forms are sufficiently different to justify calling them separate species.

It was on the Galapagos Islands that Charles Darwin observed the manner in which animals speciated (i.e., formed new species) in the isolation provided by such islands, while archipelagos (groups of islands) allow even greater speciation/subspeciation through exchange between these individual populations. In the past it has been suggested that the common occurrence of giant tortoises on islands indicated that these large forms had evolved there in the absence of predators, but it seems more probable that it may well have been that large animal species would have floated across these great water bodies far more easily than small animal species, providing a strong selection pressure for larger animals on islands.

The fact that no seafarer has ever reported seeing a large tortoise bobbing around in the ocean indicates that it must have been an uncommon event, but contemporary scientists

Below: A giant tortoise strolls across a shallow tidal pool close to Bras Takamaka.

Overleaf: On the platin *limestone of Grande Terre, tortoise turf provides the dominant element of the diet for the giant tortoises.*

have observed tortoises floating in the lagoon of Aldabra and, on one occasion, an animal was observed being swept out of Passe Houareau to the open ocean. Three features of these reptiles would have made them ideal candidates for such a mode of long-distance transportation, one being their waterproof external skeleton (with a carapace above and plastron below), and another the ability of female tortoises (and other reptiles) to store sperm for many months in small cellular crypts in their oviducts. Thus, unlike other terrestrial vertebrates, it would not have been necessary for both a male and female to arrive within the lifetime of either sex for a population to establish itself. For those who are today worried by the genetic implications of decreased numbers in endangered species, one wonders how great the chances were that the initial establishment of a tortoise population, or for that matter the other large reptiles in the past, was the result of the arrival of just one animal, which would have given rise subsequently to a whole population, unless another individual arrived in the interim. If the arrival of an animal was an unusual event, the chances of more than one arriving at the same time are very slim. The third feature was their ability to survive long periods without food, being cold-blooded animals.

Although the reasons for tortoises being washed into the sea are not clear, it is at least possible that cyclones or other tropical storms may in the past have been responsible for the

catastrophic removal of large populations of tortoises from low islands, while other individuals may simply have been swept out to sea after having floated out of mangrove swamps, where they still commonly feed on Aldabra today.

The difficult landscape of Aldabra has exerted considerable evolutionary pressures on the tortoises, which in turn have resulted in the development of a number of unique anatomical features. The Aldabra tortoise's face is quite flat and much less pointed than that of other tortoise species. This feature has been shown to be related to the ability of this animal to drink from the tiny, shallow pools which form on the surface of the coral limestone by drawing water into its nasal chamber through its nostrils. An additional feature of interest is observed in the carapace which, instead of curving downwards at the anterior end to just allow the head and forelimbs to be protruded and retracted, has a relatively large opening, exposing the skin of the neck, shoulders, and upper chest. This unique structure allows the animal to regulate its body temperature by exposing this skin to the breeze, or even to sea spray on the coast. The evolution of such a characteristic can presumably have only developed in the absence of significant predation on the adults since it would make the tortoises very vulnerable to attack by medium or large predators. Another characteristic which arouses the curiosity of those approaching a giant land tortoise for the first time is the

hissing sound it makes as it withdraws its head. The sound is, in fact, caused involuntarily by the expulsion of air from under the carapace when the head and neck are retracted.

The high temperatures and uncertain rainfall of Aldabra pose severe problems for tortoises in respect of regulating their body temperature and drinking, activities which are at least partly related. The porous nature of the coral limestone is both an advantage and a disadvantage to the water-dependent chelonians. Rain falling on the surface is quickly lost by percolation, rendering it very rapidly unavailable to the animals. The porous nature of the substrate is also an advantage, for it allows sea water from the lagoon and the sea to infiltrate the limestone, where it evaporates and then condenses in the upper layers to form a lens of fresh water which floats on the saline lower water table. During the high spring tides, this layer of fresh water is lifted to and above the limestone surface, where it replenishes large solution cavities or pools in the 'parkland' or *platin*, at the eastern end of Grande Terre. It is not, therefore, surprising that the presence of water, shade, and food are responsible for a high population density of tortoises in this area. Almost the whole of southern Grande Terre and Malabar are covered with finely dissected champignon limestone which is immensely difficult country for the tortoises; but *platin* is ideal, for it comprises large open areas of flat weathered limestone, scattered among groves of dense scrub.

If water is not directly available, animals may at least be able to satisfy some of their requirements by utilizing water in the vegetation, though during the extended dry season even the vegetation has a low water content. The survival of tortoises on the islands of Seychelles has been largely determined by the availability of water for them to drink, and since the same feature also determined whether humans would settle, or at least stay on the island for short periods, this simple ecological feature has probably played a more significant role in the extinction of tortoises in the Indian Ocean than any other. Sailing ships plying their trade in these waters would regularly call at the islands to collect tortoises, for their ability to survive for weeks or even months without water meant that they could provide a regular and reliable source of fresh meat.

The survival of a healthy population of tortoises on Aldabra is almost entirely due to the difficulties posed by the dangerous terrain of the champignon, and the almost impenetrable *Pemphis acidula* scrub which clothes it. Thus, when the tortoises had been removed from the easily accessible areas of *platin* in eastern Grande Terre it was simply not economic to spend days searching the bush for the sparse tortoise population surviving in it. We are not sure what the numbers were like at the end of the last century, but we do know that ships that visited areas where tortoises are now abundant reported that they were completely absent. It is, therefore, encouraging to see that such low population densities can recover so well when left undisturbed for nearly a century.

Studies by the Royal Society in the 1970s of the Aldabra tortoises indicated that the total population was 150,466, of which 97.7 per cent were located on Grande Terre. When expressed in terms of biomass (the number of animals multiplied by their unit weight) we observe that the optimal tortoise terrain carries between 36,347 and 58,352 kilos a square kilometre which, when set in the context of other tropical environments, is a significantly higher biomass than has ever been recorded on the large mammal-dominated savannahs of the African mainland. The fact that Aldabra is able to support such a huge biomass of tortoises is explained by the fact that large cold-blooded vertebrates experience long non-productive periods when they are exerting little effect on the level of local vegetable resources or their own reserves. In fact these amazing animals only turn over about 0.9 per cent of their biomass a year, compared with about five per cent for African elephants.

Large cold-blooded reptiles like the Aldabra tortoises maintain their body temperature close to an optimum by moving in and out of the shade during the day and resting in a sheltered place away from cooling winds at night. As the sun rises in the morning they move slowly outwards from their shelters and orient their bodies away from the sun, so that a crescentic shadow in front of the carapace protects the head from being overheated. If they are in the open towards midday and the head is no longer in the shade, as the shadow shrinks they will once more retreat into the shade until late afternoon, when they will emerge and reorientate their bodies in the opposite direction to that of the morning's period of foraging. During long bouts of feeding they will crop grasses, low herbs, dead leaves, and even carrion, with their coarse serrated beaks and blunt, rough tongues. While foraging, tortoises often show a high degree of selectivity in their feeding, taking, for instance, the inflorescences of grasses during the flowering season. Their gut contributes 16.7 per cent and its contents twelve per cent (jointly 28.7 per cent) of an animal's body weight, indicating that these large cold-blooded reptiles retain their food as long as they possibly can (in order to extract as much nutriment as possible), in their otherwise rather inefficient digestive system.

When animals live in comparatively simple ecosystems there are far fewer checks and balances imposed by their potential competitors and predators. Aldabra is such a system, for the giant tortoise is the only significant herbivore, although in recent years goats brought to the atoll by human settlers have begun to compete with the reptiles at the eastern end of Grande Terre. An eradication programme funded by the World Bank was begun in 1993/94 with the aim of eliminating goats from Aldabra, although this remains a daunting task. Except during periods of severe drought, the tortoise population can be expected to rise until demand on their food resources exceeds supply. What we observe today is that the tortoises stop growing at an early stage in their lives, due to a shortage of food within their normal foraging range, a situation that has probably happened, possibly cyclically, many times in the past. They are opportunistic scavengers and have been known to eat the flesh of other, dead, tortoises. The World Bank-funded goat killers even found on several occasions that, having shot a goat, by the time they reached the corpse a tortoise was already licking blood from the fresh wound.

Provided animals are willing and able to move within their normal habitat range, it is likely that they will be able to utilize some food resources which are available when others

Below: Goats introduced by man for food are now being eradicated to prevent competition with the endemic giant land tortoise.

are in short supply. On Aldabra, it has been discovered that some of the tortoises living inland undertake annual movements to the coast to feed on the coarse *Sporobolus* grasslands on the coastal beaches, when inland food was in short supply. Such a local migration is probably timed to coincide with the first rain, which washes the salt off the coastal vegetation, and when the inland vegetation has not yet responded to the advent of rain with a growth spurt. It seems possible that the females undergoing such a migration would have better resources for egg-laying than their counterparts which have remained inland, even though the lack of shade on the coast presents a much greater risk of dying from heat stroke when foraging in the open.

As in all ecosystems, it is invariably the quality rather than the quantity of available food which influences much of the feeding behaviour and movements of local animal populations. In the case of Aldabra we are able to see a very exciting example of the huge influence that a herbivore can have on the local vegetation. On the *platin* limestone of Grande Terre there is a low vegetation type which occupies shallow eroded depressions in the surface. This vegetation community is called tortoise turf, for it provides the dominant vegetable element (sixty-one per cent of feeding observations) of the tortoise diet. Additionally, feeding trials have revealed that it passes through the gut much quicker than

the coarse *Sporobolus* grass of the coast. The discovery of tortoise turf was of great evolutionary interest for it revealed that this low sward is made up of a complex of six genera of grasses/sedges and at least four genera of low dicotyledonous herbs. The low growth form (no more than two centimetres) has been shown to be a community of genetic dwarfs which have evolved under continuous pressure from grazing tortoises. Thus, unlike the garden lawn, which will grow quite tall if it is not mown, the tortoise turf will remain short even in the absence of grazing. Recent experiments have demonstrated that this vegetation type only persists in the presence of the tortoises, for if they are excluded, other more vigorous (mainly grass and sedge) species quickly displace the turf. Indeed it seems probable that the extinction of tortoises on other Indian Ocean islands has led to the loss of most of these plant species, except for small patches on very shallow soils, where their competitors cannot establish themselves.

The most significant features of any animal's behaviour are its ability to breed and its success at breeding. Giant tortoise mating takes place on Aldabra from January to May. It is a noisy affair; the bellow of the male tortoise is commonly heard in the early morning and late afternoon during this period. The male has a concave plastron to facilitate the task of mounting the female, which has a flat plastron. The male can also be identified by its longer,

thinner tail. Aldabra tortoises lay their eggs from late June until late September, with a peak in July. The eggs are buried in the soil and incubation may vary from ninety-eight to 148 days, with the longer incubation periods being recorded for those eggs laid early in the season. From examinations of animals on Aldabra, it is clear that tortoises in the dense population of Grande Terre mature later (twenty-three years) than those on Malabar (seventeen years). When we study populations we are interested in determining the manner in which local resource levels influence recruitment. We believe that the lack of growth on Grande Terre could be caused by a shortage of food, and that this shortage could also be expected to influence recruitment.

Studies of breeding on Aldabra entailed field researchers locating nests and then recording the number of eggs per clutch, the size of individual eggs, and the body mass of hatchlings. These data immediately indicated that there was a striking inverse relationship between the density of animals on an island and the numbers of eggs laid per nest (i.e., the denser the population the less resources are available for each animal, which in consequence can lay fewer eggs). The results revealed that in 1976 the animals on Grande Terre laid 5.3 eggs per nest, those on Malabar 14.0 eggs per nest, while those on Picard (where many of the tortoises have been introduced) 19.2 eggs per nest. The respective animal densities for

*Below: Wallowing in shallow pools provides vital cooling
for giant tortoises.*

these clutch sizes were twenty-seven, seven, and five animals per hectare. Such a clear relationship indicates a probable connection between clutch size, tortoise density, and the level of available food resources. A much stronger line of evidence emerged when the comparative data between 1975 and 1976 were examined, and demonstrated that a forty-three per cent increase in rainfall in 1976 resulted in a twenty-three per cent increase in mean clutch size (5.3 eggs per clutch in 1976, compared with 4.2 eggs in 1975, the drier year) for the Grande Terre population. Since the additional rain had fallen at the beginning of the breeding season it appears that, although the animals are normally food-limited, additional forage at the time of egg-laying leads to an immediate increase in clutch size. Dissected animals revealed that at the onset of breeding the ovaries possess sufficient developing ova to lay a theoretically full clutch (about thirty eggs), but if their internal food reserves are poor they begin to resorb some of the immature ova so that they may fully provision the small complement of each egg which is finally laid. Thus, it seems that the level of local food resources acts as a means of controlling tortoise numbers through its internal control over clutch size.

Once a new generation of tortoises emerges from the ground they are faced by all the dangers posed by living on a rugged coral atoll. The little pockets of soil in the the limestone

*Below: The empty, bleached shells of dead giant tortoises are
an ever-present reminder that life is tough on Aldabra.
Overleaf: Plumes of spray mist over a golden sunset.*

foster collections of small plants which are ideal for young tortoises to feed on, but they are potential prey for a number of local predators. Both the eggs and hatchlings are taken in fairly large numbers by the coconut or robber crab and the mangrove crab, while the pied crows and sacred ibis also take their toll. On Malabar the endemic white-throated rail has also learned how to kill and eat hatchlings by spearing them through the old egg sac opening on the plastron (the ventral shell). Beyond the hatchling stage they are fairly immune to such predation and the major causes of mortality for the immature and adult stages are through dying, isolated away from shade on the coastal grasslands, from heat stroke, or through falling down one of the many steep-sided pits in the champignon.

The age of a giant land tortoise can be measured from growth rings on the scutes or scales of the carapace for the first ten to fifteen years, in much the same way that trees can be aged. However, in order to know the age of individual tortoises after they have passed fifteen years, the Royal Society developed a method of attaching numbered titanium discs to the carapace (titanium does not rust) so that specific tortoises can be identified and their growth monitored. Size (including weight) is a function of how much food there is and the population density. Tortoises on Grande Terre stop growing very early in life and even the largest ones probably do not reach more than forty kilos. On Malabar, however, where they

are not crowded, they probably closely approach 100 kilos and, in the past, before they were preyed on by humans, they probably achieved even greater sizes. Animals introduced to Picard more than doubled their weight and size in a few years, but as numbers have increased that rate of growth has slowed down. Sexual maturity also depends on the population density, and Aldabran giant tortoises, in theory, can probably continue to breed throughout life, but this depends on how much food they are getting.

Stories of the great age achieved by tortoises are often exaggerated though, according to *The Guinness Book of Records*, the greatest authentic age recorded for a chelonian is over 152 years, for a male Marion's tortoise brought from Seychelles to Mauritius in 1766 by Chevalier du Fresne, who presented it to the Port Louis army garrison. It went blind in 1908 and was accidently killed in 1918. A second entry in *The Guinness Book of Records* for the largest living tortoise is that of a male Aldabra giant land tortoise resident on Bird Island, Seychelles, which weighed in at 304 kilos. In the truly wild and difficult conditions of Aldabra, such great age and size is unlikely to be reached.

The giant tortoise population of Aldabra provides a superb and unparalleled field laboratory to study the factors which affect and control animal numbers. In spite of the many years that these animals have been studied, many of the more intriguing questions remain unanswered. Sadly, increasing costs have reduced the number of scientists who are able and willing to go to this remote spot in the Indian Ocean, where their presence is also a reminder that a World Heritage Site does not look after itself but needs continuing care, attention, and protection. In 1994, the World Bank funded the employment of two Research Officers (thanks to the Global Environment Facility initiative), in an endeavour to revive the research programmes that this unique atoll merits. No doubt Aldabra and its tortoises will continue to yield a fascinating wealth of information.

6

'BIRDS OF ALMOST ALL DESCRIPTION'

ADRIAN SKERRETT

*'The birds are tame, entirely trusting, as vulnerable to the sticks of men as the great slow tortoise.
Under the clear gaze of such creatures, in this bright whispering wood, there comes a painful memory
of Eden.'*
BLUE MERIDIAN
Peter Matthiessen

*Above: The male Aldabran fody in its distinctive breeding
plumage.*

To THE BIRDWATCHER, ALDABRA IS A living legend. When ninety per cent of bird extinctions during the last 300 years have been island forms; when almost all islands of the Indian Ocean are dominated by introduced birds; when large seabird colonies have been decimated or destroyed elsewhere; when two thirds of today's endangered species are on islands much altered by man; when flightless birds have disappeared from every other corner of the Indian Ocean; Aldabra lives on. Little has changed. Certainly man's influence, including his habit of introducing predators such as rats and cats, has touched Aldabra's avifauna, but the damage has not been terminal.

If you are a birdwatcher lucky enough to visit Aldabra, you can anticipate the excitement of discovering 'lifers'; new species for your life list. Yet coming from Mahé, the first impression is one of familiarity. There is a fody, a sunbird, a bulbul, a white-eye, and a turtle dove. Look again, for these are not the species of the central Seychelles, and much greater differences lie just around the corner.

Perhaps the first bird you encounter, the red-headed forest fody or Aldabran fody (*Foudia eminentissima aldabrana*), is a unique Aldabra subspecies, unlike the Madagascar fody found throughout central Seychelles and the Amirantes, which is introduced. Fodies are confined in their natural state to the western Indian Ocean, and the red-headed forest fody evolved either in Madagascar or in Comoros, from where Aldabra was colonized.

The genus comprises five species (or perhaps six if the Aldabran fody is treated as a full species) and ten subspecies, which vary considerably in the size and shape of the bill, according to diet. Aldabran fodies feed both on small insects and other invertebrates and on seeds. They are acrobatic birds and may climb tree trunks or hang upside down to feed under leaves. Dead leaves may be torn apart in the search for insects, or the tips of dead twigs snapped off and examined, and they also feed on nectar.

All fodies are sexually dimorphic, i.e., the males and females differ in size, colour, patterning, etc. Breeding males of the Aldabran fody are scarlet on the upper breast, head, nape, and much of the upper parts, and yellow on the lower breast. The black bill merges into a black stripe through the eye. Females and immature males are much duller; somewhat sparrow-like at first glance, they are pale olive-green above and yellowish olive below, with a pale bill and eyebrow. The Aldabran fody breeds between December and March when rainfall produces an abundance of insect prey and casuarina seeds. The circular nest is often built high in coconut or casuarina trees; this is probably a recent development as both these tree species may be introduced, and research suggests that it was possibly in response to predation by the introduced rats, which take a heavy toll of eggs and nestlings.

Similar origins can be attributed to the Souimanga sunbird (*Nectarinia sovimanga aldabraensis*), although, curiously, whereas the fody genus is believed to have earlier African roots, the sunbird genus is probably of Asian stock. There is a startling similarity between the under parts of the male Souimanga sunbird and the olive-back sunbird (*N. jugularis*), which has itself evolved into more than a score of subspecies throughout South-East Asia and Indonesia. Strangely enough, elsewhere within the Aldabran group of islands,

Below: The adult male lesser frigatebird endeavours to impress potential mates with its balloon-like scarlet throat patch inflated.

Bottom: Frigatebirds cannot land on water as they are equipped with poor waterproofing. If they do so accidentally, they are unable to take off again.

centuries of isolation have produced two other separate subspecies of the Souimanga sunbird, *N.S abbotti* on Assumption and *N.S buchenorum* on Cosmoledo and possibly Astove.

Breeding males perch in the open and sing loudly; they display to other birds with the chest thrust out and bill raised almost to vertical. The breeding season starts earlier than other landbirds, in August, and continues to April. The earlier start may be in response to nectar abundance, whereas other Aldabran birds depend more on insects. Outside the breeding season, flocks of up to thirty birds may be seen chasing one another through the trees and calling excitedly.

Malagasy turtle doves (*Streptopelia picturata coppingeri*) are fairly common around the buildings of the settlement and Research Station, searching for seeds on the ground in open areas. Endemic to the western Indian Ocean, the Malagasy turtle dove has evolved into a number of different forms as far afield as Diego Garcia. Two other forms found in Seychelles — *S.p rostrata* in central Seychelles and *S.p aldabrana* in the Amirantes — are threatened with elimination from hybridization due to the unnecessary introduction of Malagasy turtle doves of the nominate form from outside the region. Fortunately, there is no such threat on Aldabra, where nature has been allowed to take its own course. This is one of the wonders and attractions of Aldabra's avifauna: unlike almost any other island of any significant size in the Indian Ocean, there are no introduced bird species to compete with the indigenous forms.

The Malagasy bulbul (*Hypsipetes madagascariensis rostratus*) is also endemic to Aldabra. The plumage differences between bulbuls of the Malagasy region (there are subspecies on Iles Glorieuses, Madagascar, and Comoros) are extremely slight and it is possible that they all evolved from relatively recent colonization by Asian black bulbuls. It may even be that there was a simultaneous colonization of the entire region, rather than colonization on Aldabra and elsewhere by Madagascan birds.

The fifth common land bird is the Malagasy white-eye (*Zosterops maderaspatana aldabraensis*). The nominate race from Madagascar also probably belongs to the same form found on Iles Glorieuses, Astove, and possibly Cosmoledo (though some authorities separate this as *menaiensis*). Unlike the Seychelles grey white-eye (*Zosterops modesta*), found in only small numbers in the mountains of Mahé, the Malagasy white-eye is relatively common. Small family parties or groups of up to thirty birds flit through the vegetation almost everywhere, though they appear to have a marked preference for mangroves and casuarina groves.

To seek out other unique land birds of Aldabra usually requires exploration of the paths that radiate from the settlement. The low cooing of the Comoro blue pigeon (*Alectroenas sganzini minor*) betrays the presence of one of the most beautiful birds of the atoll. Blue pigeons were recorded as plentiful on Farquhar and Providence in 1821–1822, but sadly these were gone even before it was known whether they were similar to the birds of Aldabra or to the Seychelles blue pigeon (*Alectroenas pulcherrima*) of central Seychelles. They are never seen feeding on the ground and this prevents competition with the turtle doves which

Below: Greater flamingo are elusive but may sometimes be seen in the south-eastern corner of the atoll.

Overleaf: The greater flamingo was found to breed on Aldabra as recently as 1995. The atoll is the only oceanic breeding site for this species, apart from the Galapagos.

feed mostly on the ground on seeds and small invertebrate animals.

The strangest call of any of the land birds of Aldabra is that of the Malagasy coucal (*Centropus toulou insularis*) or black coucal. This reluctant flier skulks in the undergrowth or runs along branches to the treetops, whence it repeats a deep gurgling call which sounds very much like a water bottle being emptied. Chestnut and black when in breeding plumage, with a long tail (longer than the nominate form from Madagascar), the Malagasy coucal builds an oval nest in which three or four white eggs are laid. It feeds mainly on arthropods such as insects and on geckos and skinks, using its heavy beak to prise open tree bark and to search in crevices.

Though uncommon, it may not require quite so much searching to find the Malagasy kestrel (*Falco newtoni*). It may find you! For many years, a pair nested in an artificial nest box erected on one of the settlement buildings. Pass too close to the building and the male would swoop down on the offending person and strike them on the back of the head with its talons, then alight nearby, fixing the intruder with a stare that left no doubt as to whom the territory belonged. Unlike most other land birds of the atoll, the Malagasy kestrel has not evolved into an identifiably separate form. The first record of this species on the atoll was in 1878 and possibly it may not be much before this date that it became established

here. Too little time has passed for unique Aldabra characteristics to have developed, but who knows what the future may hold? However, it is by no means common and only time will tell whether it continues to breed here or suffers the same fate as the barn owl (*Tyto alba*), which colonized Aldabra, almost certainly by natural means, from Madagascar or the Comoros, and then mysteriously vanished for unknown reasons. In 1892, Dr Abbott found the barn owl 'rather common'. By the early part of the twentieth century, it had gone.

Apart from the kestrel, the only other land bird of Aldabra inseparable from forms found elsewhere is the pied crow (*Corvus albus*). Pied crows are widespread throughout the Afro-Malagasy region, and are also found on Madagascar, Comoros, Iles Glorieuses, and Assumption. On Aldabra, they range over the whole atoll, acting in their usual role of scavengers, and nesting in the tall casuarina trees. Despite misguided attempts at one time to control them, in the belief that they may have been introduced and that their population might be increasing to the point where they began to become a danger to some of the rarer species of Aldabra, they form a natural element of the indigenous avifauna.

The Malagasy nightjar (*Caprimulgus asiaticus aldabraensis*) is difficult to locate. It relies on its cryptic colouring to remain invisible among the leaf litter, emerging in the evening to search for flying insects. However, if you do manage to find one, it is often possible to approach very closely indeed, since they remain still, in the belief that their camouflage is perfect. The races of birds from the Malagasy region and India are remarkably similar, though Malagasy forms lack the golden collar on the nape of Indian birds.

The inland woodland is also the habitat of the most distinctive bird to be found on most of Aldabra, the Aldabra drongo (*Dicrurus aldabranus*). Unlike all the other land birds mentioned thus far, this is undisputed as a completely separate species, most likely derived from the crested drongo of Madagascar, from which it has now diverged to a considerable degree. As well as plumage differences, the call is also distinctive. Fairly common throughout the atoll, the population is about 1,500 birds.

Family parties of about four birds feed together, pouncing on lizards or large insects. They are aggressive birds and have been seen to mob Aldabran fruit bats and birds larger than themselves, including pied crow, Malagasy kestrel and green-backed heron.

Another species unique to Aldabra is, according to the *ICBP/IUCN Red Data Book* 'almost certainly the rarest, most restricted and most highly threatened species of bird in the world'. This is the Aldabra brush warbler (*Nesillas aldabranus*). Indeed, it may sadly be too late to save this species from extinction. Discovered only in 1968, all but one on record are from a fifty-metre-wide strip of land covering ten hectares on Malabar. Introduced cats and rats may have already claimed this species as a victim, though given the difficulty of exploring the terrain, and the availability of suitable habitat elsewhere, such as on Grande Terre, there is still a glimmer of hope that one day the Aldabra brush warbler may be rediscovered.

Sightings were regular, although sparse, through the 1970s, but the last sighting was in September 1983. If the species is now extinct, it is difficult to pinpoint the cause, but rats must be a prime suspect. The only nest ever found was deep in a spiky pandanus tree, not

*Top left: Endemic to the western Indian Ocean, Malagasy
turtle doves have evolved into a number of different forms,
including one which is unique to Aldabra. Centre left: The Malagasy coucal
runs along trunks and branches to the treetops, from where it
emits a deep gurgling call. Bottom left: Crested terns breed on at least seven
islets in the lagoon.
Top right: A speciality of coral atolls, the black-naped tern.
On Aldabra it favours breeding sites on small islets linking the
lagoon and the open ocean. Centre right: Its cryptic colouring and nocturnal
habits make the Malagasy nightjar a most difficult bird to locate,
but at dusk its call can be heard throughout the interior of the atoll.
Bottom right: Immature frigatebirds grow slowly, taking up to seven
months to fledge.*

Top left: Brown noddies breed colonially on many of the small lagoon islets. Centre left: The Aldabra drongo is a distinctive bird, and, unlike most of the land birds, is a unique species. Bottom left: A juvenile green-backed heron explores the shoreline at low tide. Top right: Green-backed herons are common along the shoreline, both inside and outside the lagoon. Centre right: The Malagasy bulbul, an endemic sub-species, feeds on berries close to the Research Station. Bottom right: Though flightless, the white-throated rail will occasionally clamber on to branches up to one metre from the ground.

easily penetrated by rats. Perhaps also the species evolved in conditions that have since changed and, when first discovered, it had only a precarious hold on its survival. It may be that we have, unknowingly, witnessed a natural species extinction.

The most fascinating and alluring of all the birds of Aldabra atoll is the white-throated rail or Aldabra rail (*Dryolimnas cuvieri aldabranus*), the last surviving flightless bird of the Indian Ocean, a region once famous for its flightless forms. The common dodo (*Raphus cucullatus*) has gone. This, undoubtedly the largest and strangest dove that ever existed, was once the jewel in the crown of the rich avifauna of Mauritius. Unaccustomed to predators, the dodo never knew fear, and was slaughtered for sport. The flesh was reputed to be bitter and tough, but the introduction of pigs, monkeys, rats and cats sealed the fate of the dodo, and by 1693, almost a century before the first settlement in Seychelles, it was gone. Likewise, the Reunion solitaire (*Raphus solitarius*) was extinct by 1746 and the Rodriguez solitaire (*Pezophaps solitaria*) between 1761 and 1791.

Some of the most incredible birds the world has ever known were also flightless birds of the Indian Ocean, the elephant birds (*Aepyornithidae*). Though they were wiped out by man before Europeans rounded the Cape of Good Hope, these birds inspired legends, possibly the most famous of which was that of the roc, which Sinbad the Sailor encountered on his fifth epic voyage. Sinbad's roc could fly and, enraged by the destruction of its egg by merchants accompanying Sinbad, dropped stones on his ship, sending it, and many of its crew, to the ocean depths.

So much for the roc's revenge. The reality is that man's destruction of birds and their habitats proceeded at breakneck pace following the colonization of the region, and only the white-throated rail survived, thanks to the isolation of Aldabra. Rails are one of the world's oldest and most widespread bird families, found everywhere except the polar regions. As they feed and nest on the ground, rarely flying unless forced to do so, they are prime candidates for evolving into flightless birds. Indeed, not just in the Aldabra group did they occur in the Indian Ocean. The Mauritian red rail (*Aphanapteryx bonasia*) disappeared around the same time as the dodo, according to Francois Cauche, due to the fact that 'to capture them one need only show them a scrap of red cloth which they then pursue and let themselves be seized in your hand'. This became a popular sport until there were no more rails left. A similar fascination for the colour red led to the extinction of Legaut's rail (*Aphanapteryx leguati*) on nearby Rodriguez and to rails on other islands in the Aldabra group.

The white-throated rail on Aldabra is one of the most appealing birds because of its behaviour. It is extremely curious and will emerge from the bushes to investigate any strange noise. The traditional way of attracting them is to tap two sticks together. Once they have emerged from the thick vegetation in which they normally live, they become even more curious and will often approach to within a few inches in order to investigate. Their calls are extremely loud and carry over long distances (over a kilometre) and consist of assorted clicks, booming sounds, and long-drawn-out wails. Often, a pair will 'sing'

*Below: The red-footed booby is often attacked by
frigatebirds which will attempt to steal its catch, yet the two species
coexist in the mangrove breeding colonies.*

together and, if this occurs when you are close to them, it can be almost deafening. For a bird weighing only two or three hundred grams, it is an extraordinary performance.

They nest on or near the ground and are vigorous in the defence of their three to five eggs and of their young. Approached by a human, they will first threaten by spreading their wings and screaming and, if this doesn't frighten you off, they will often stab at your feet or legs with their beaks.

Today, the rails are limited to Malabar, Polymnie, and two of the larger lagoon islets, although it is not known if they have ever really established themselves elsewhere on the atoll. The surviving population of several thousand is healthy and, given the continued protection of Aldabra, the last flightless bird of the Indian Ocean can look forward to a secure future.

The breeding season for almost all the thirteen land bird species of Aldabra starts from around October to December, when the onset of the north-west monsoon rains brings an abundance of food for feeding young birds. Some species nest earlier than this, notably the kestrel and the nightjar, the young of which need to develop hunting skills during the wet season.

Returning to the shoreline, you may think it unlikely that special Aldabra forms would be found among the shore birds, which are more likely to travel between separate landmasses, or be blown out to sea during the periods of strong winds. You would be wrong. The Aldabran sacred ibis (*Threskiornis aethiopica abbotti*) differs from the African form, not just in plumage, but also in having distinctive Wedgwood blue eyes. Strangely enough, an adult sacred ibis of the nominate race was recorded on Aldabra on 23rd February 1968, proof of the ability of this species to cross the ocean to Aldabra. The ibis of Aldabra is most similar to *T. a. bernieri* of Madagascar. Dr W.L. Abbott, who visited Aldabra in 1892, collected the first specimen, which Robert Ridgway, writing in 1895, considered was probably an insular form and proposed the name *Ibis abbotti*. Abbott found the *corbiz blan* (as it is known in Creole) 'common and extremely tame. A half dozen birds live constantly about the camp, feeding upon scraps and turtle offal'.

Only on Aldabra, Madagascar and Iles Glorieuses does the dimorphic egret (*Egretta dimorpha*) breed. Regarded by some authorities not as a separate species but merely a race of little egret (*Egretta garzetta*) which colonized the region from Africa, both black and white forms occur here. It is strange that neither the Comoros nor central Seychelles has ever been colonized by this species. Although little egrets sometimes occur as migrants in central Seychelles, no black forms have ever been seen there, indicating that wherever it is they come from, it is unlikely to be Aldabra.

Dr Abbott estimated the white form to be two or three times more numerous than the black. He found them breeding in the mangroves during his December 1892 visit, when 'at low tide this and other species of herons, with curlews and sandpipers, feed upon the fringing reef in thousands; then as the tide rises the whole crowd fly over into the lagoon, where the tide is one or two hours later, and continue feeding there until the water becomes too deep.'

Aldabra is also the only breeding site in Seychelles for the Malagasy squacco heron (*Ardeola idae*). There are probably less than 100 birds, which occur mainly at the eastern end of the lagoon, although their rather secretive habits make it difficult to estimate the size of the breeding population. Colonization may have been very recent. Abbott, who spent more than three months at Aldabra in 1892, did not see this species.

Other breeding shore birds are the grey heron (*Ardea cinerea*), cattle egret (*Bubulcus ibis*), and green-backed heron (*Butorides striatus*). It is curious that the last of these is of the race *B.s. crawfordi*, believed to be of Asian origin, whereas the race found in the granitics, *B.s. degens*, seems likely to be of African origin. Dr Abbott observed: 'They are extremely fond of bluebottle flies, which swarm upon the backs and heads of the turtles when on shore. They stand by hours upon the turtle's back, darting out their beaks with unerring aim upon the blood-sucking flies.' On Aldabra, they have certainly expanded their feeding niche since they are often seen away from the shoreline, well inland in the scrub and woodland, feeding on large insects, geckos and skinks.

The greater flamingo (*Phoenicopterus ruber*) deserves special mention. It has been seen in flocks of up to 500 birds on Aldabra. A single egg was found in 1967, but there was no other evidence of breeding until the discovery in 1995 of a small nesting colony and a chick, not yet able to fly. This exciting find means Aldabra is the only coral atoll in the world where this species breeds. Indeed, the only other oceanic breeding site in the world is the Galapagos. It is still not known whether breeding is annual or sporadic, but the ability of Aldabra to continue to surprise the scientific world is undoubtedly a measure of its inestimable value.

Excluding the flamingo, the origins of which are uncertain, it is interesting that, despite the proximity of the African continent, just one Aldabran breeding bird, the dimorphic egret, originates from there. Of the other eighteen land and shore birds, seventeen can, not so surprisingly, be ascribed to the Malagasy region, which is not only very close, but also lies in the direction of the south-east winds, which blow for half the year. More surprising is how many species have earlier origins in Asia. Perhaps they colonized during a time of much lower sea levels, assisted by the north-west monsoon winds.

Apart from its rich and unique avifauna of land birds and shore birds, Aldabra atoll boasts some of the greatest sea bird colonies on earth. Pride of place must go to the most conspicuous of all, the frigatebirds with their two-metre wingspan. Two species breed there, the great frigatebird (*Fregata minor*) and the lesser frigatebird (*Fregata ariel*), with 4,000 pairs and 6,000 pairs respectively. This combined population makes Aldabra one of the largest frigatebird breeding sites in the world. Only McKean Island in the Pacific Ocean, with 15,000 breeding pairs, is known to be of greater size.

Frigatebirds breed along the inner northern rim of the atoll, especially on Malabar. They have the most spectacular courtship display of any sea bird. The male bird sets up his post, often in old, disused nests among the mangroves. He spreads and inverts his wings, inflates his bright scarlet throat patch like a balloon, throws his head back, the bill pointing to the sky, and quivers with excitement in an endeavour to impress potential mates flying overhead. In the case of the great frigatebird, this is accompanied by a loud, resonant call. Eventually, a female succumbs to this hypnotic ritual and descends to join in the performance. They rub necks and the male may hold the female's bill in his own and, over the next two or three days, the bond is established.

An untidy nest is built from twigs, feathers and seaweed, in which a single egg is laid. Nests are grouped together, almost always in mangroves, with about twenty nests to a group. Both sexes take part in incubation, each sitting on the egg for periods of between one and four days (although a period of up to eighteen days has been recorded). The chick hatches after about fifty days and is guarded for the first month of its life by each adult in turn. They grow very slowly, taking up to seven months to fledge. Post-fledging parental care is the longest of any sea bird and, in great frigatebirds, can sometimes last as long as eighteen months. Consequently, they may not breed every year. The failure rate is also high, at seventy-five per cent, and birds do not reach maturity until seven or more years of age. To compensate, frigatebirds are long-lived, the record known age being thirty-four years.

Frigatebirds are notorious as pirates of the air, chasing and harrying tropicbirds, boobies, and other seabirds to force them to drop or regurgitate their catches. Using their tails as rudders they perform astonishing aerobatics, to knock their victims off balance and frighten

Top left: The red-footed booby has a population of up to 3,000 pairs. Birds rove far out to sea in search of food. Centre left: An adult crested tern, silhouetted against the sky, as it searches the shallow lagoon waters for small fish. Bottom left: The Aldabran sacred ibis differs from the African form in plumage and in having distinctive Wedgwood blue eyes.
Top right: Crab plovers are equipped with heavy bills enabling them to snap up small crabs or dismember and consume larger prey. Centre right: Pied crows have reached many islands of the western Indian Ocean by natural means, including Aldabra. Bottom right: Though they are maestros of flight, the short legs of frigatebirds are useless for walking, enabling them merely to perch where they land.

them into giving up their catch. However, more than eighty per cent of their food is caught directly, their speed enabling them to even outmanoeuvre flying fish, so piratical attacks are probably only a minor source of food. In fact, as frigatebirds greatly outnumber boobies at Aldabra, it would not be possible for the frigatebirds to survive on food from their piracy.

Due to this evolutionary emphasis on aerial superiority, the legs and feet have become stunted, so that frigatebirds can barely walk or swim. They are primitive birds with poor waterproofing compared with other seabirds, so they cannot land on the water for any length of time as they would quickly become waterlogged.

Little is known of the movements of the Aldabran frigatebirds outside the breeding season. One lesser frigatebird chick tagged in 1969 was found near Bombay in June 1970, a distance of about 4,400 kilometres. Non-breeding frigatebirds can be seen commonly elsewhere in Seychelles, notably at Coetivy and Aride, 1,200km from Aldabra. Many non-breeding birds can be seen the year round on Aldabra and the atoll's population at the peak of the breeding season may be as high as 27,000 frigatebirds. The sight of these enormous but amazingly agile flying machines, rising in clouds over Aldabra, is truly spectacular and must be considered as one of the world's natural wonders.

Breeding in the mangroves alongside the frigatebirds are the red-footed boobies (*Sula sula*). They build a flimsy nest of twigs bound together by droppings in which a single egg is laid. Incubation takes about six weeks. Boobies have no brood patch, and they incubate their eggs by standing on them. Immediately after hatching, the chick is placed on the webbed feet of the parents for the first few days. Like the frigatebirds, fledging is fairly lengthy (about four months), and further parental care can last more than six months. Maturity is reached at two or three years of age. Also like frigatebirds, they are long-lived, the greatest age known being twenty-three years.

The largest colonies are between Ile Verte and Passe Houareau, and at Bras Takamaka and Johnny Channel. The total population is probably around 4,000 to 5,000 pairs. Most lay their eggs during the wet north-west monsoon (October to March), although some colonies may have a secondary peak during the late dry season.

Apart from the frigate and booby colonies, only one other sea bird species nests in trees on the atoll. This is the delightful fairy tern (*Gygis alba*) which on Aldabra also favours the mangroves growing widely around the lagoon, except for those on the southern inner rim. Some fairy terns also breed along the outer rim of the atoll on Malabar, Polymnie, at Gionnet and at Passe Femme islets on the western lagoon edge. Laying is concentrated between September and March, and the fairy tern must win the prize for the most precarious nest sites of all birds since, although a few pairs breed on bare ground, the majority balance their single egg on a horizontal branch or in a tree fork or knot hole.

Fairy terns are often remarkably curious and will approach humans to get a closer look. When doing this, they fly in their buoyant fashion to within a few metres and then hover right in front of you, as if posing for a photograph.

The same preference for breeding during the months of the north-west monsoon is seen

in the other two tern species which feed beyond the reef edge, the black-naped tern (*Stenna sumatrana*) and the brown noddy (*Anous stolidus*). In this respect, Aldabra is, once again, different from the central Seychelles, where brown noddies breed mainly from March to October, as do all roseate terns, lesser noddies, and sooty terns. The most likely reasons for this difference are the seasonal changes in ocean currents and the migration of predatory tuna on which these species depend to chase smaller fish close to the surface, within reach of the terns. Those on Aldabra time their breeding so that they are feeding their young at the time when most food is available, i.e., when the tuna shoals are present.

The favoured breeding sites for black-naped terns are almost exclusively small islets close to the channels linking the lagoon and the sea. Usually just one pair breeds on any islet, the maximum recorded on one islet being three pairs. The total breeding population is probably in the region of seventy pairs. Nests are usually on bare rock, occasionally with a few twigs or broken snail shells and leaves, in which one or two eggs are laid.

Brown noddies also favour islets, but are colonial breeders with up to 600 pairs recorded on one islet at Coffee Camp. Nests are built from sea grass, twigs and leaves, often in slight depressions where usually a single egg is laid (though nests with two eggs or chicks have sometimes been found).

The other two species of tern which breed on Aldabra feed exclusively in shallow reef or lagoon waters. The Caspian tern (*Sterna caspia*) and crested tern (*Thalasseus bergii*) both breed during the south-east monsoon, although the crested tern also lays in December and January.

The Caspian tern has its main colony on Iles Moustique, with breeding also recorded on Esprit and perhaps on Ile Michel. Aldabra is thought to be the only oceanic breeding site in the world for this species. However, the number of birds involved is very small, being somewhere in the low tens. One or two eggs are laid close to the high tide mark, so close in fact that nests are sometimes lost to high spring tides.

Crested terns breed on at least seven islets within the lagoon with a population of perhaps 150 birds. No nest is built, one egg (very occasionally two) being laid on bare rock or grass.

Two of the world's three species of tropicbird breed on Aldabra. The red-tailed tropicbird (*Phaethon rubricauda*), absent from central Seychelles except for a few pairs on Aride, has a healthy population of about 1,800 pairs on Aldabra, on small lagoon islets where they nest on the ground in the shade of bushes or tussock grass. White-tailed tropicbirds (*Phaethon lepturus*) also breed all the year round, with a population of around 2,400 pairs, favouring solution holes below the rock surface to lay their single egg. Both species feed on flying fish and squid, though the red-tailed tropicbird takes larger fish and relatively fewer squid, thus avoiding competition for food to some extent.

On land, tropicbirds are awkward and ungainly. Their feet and legs are too small for them to stand up, so that they shuffle along on their bellies. In flight they are wonderfully graceful birds. Their long tail feathers may help them to manoeuvre and are also used in display. White-tailed tropicbirds are strong fliers, often travelling huge distances in search of food (which they capture by plunge-diving), while red-tailed tropicbirds are less pelagic, seeking their food mainly in the waters around the atoll.

Tropicbirds lay a single egg. Chicks grow slowly, but reach adult weight around halfway through the nesting period of about ninety days. Towards the end of this period, parental visits become less frequent until eventually the chicks venture out to take their first flight. Unlike the frigatebirds and boobies, tropicbirds are immediately independent upon fledging.

Both species breed throughout the year, although the red-tailed tropicbirds' cycle is more synchronized, with peaks during the first four months of the year (the rainy season), and troughs during August/September (the driest months), when heat stress may deter them from nesting.

Shearwaters, a large group of seabirds, spread throughout the oceans of the world, are represented on Aldabra by just one species, the Audubon's shearwater (*Puffinus lherminieri*). They spend most of their time at sea, leaving at dawn and returning after dusk, a habit which explains why it was only as recently as 1967–1968 that breeding on the atoll was confirmed. Again, a single egg is laid. Incubation takes about fifty days, and fledging a further seventy days. One bird ringed as an adult is known to have lived for at least eleven years.

Apart from the resident breeding birds, Aldabra is also a fascinating place to see migrant birds, some of which have never been recorded anywhere else in Seychelles, such as the African darter (*Anhinga rufa*) and hoopoe (*Upupa epops*), while others are probably annual, such as barn swallow (*Hirundo rustica*), wheatear (*Oenanthe oenanthe*), and broad-billed roller (*Eurystomus glaucurus*). Along the shoreline and on exposed mud and sand banks in the lagoon, crab plovers (*Dromas ardeola*) are a common sight, often in huge flocks, and Eleonora's falcons (*Falco eleonorae*) frequently pass through en route from their breeding grounds in the Mediterranean to their Madagascar wintering quarters.

Aldabra may be a vital link for some migrant birds. It is certainly a vital island for sea birds, with more breeding species than anywhere else in Seychelles, while its unique collection of island subspecies and complete lack of introduced competitors is unrivalled anywhere in the Indian Ocean. Despite rats, cats and goats and despite the humans who brought them all in the first place, Aldabra's avifauna has survived virtually intact. Islands are often the most fragile of environments but also arguably the most fascinating. So many have been laid irrevocably to waste even before their avifauna had been properly documented, but not Aldabra. Therein lies its importance both scientific and aesthetic. We must also regard it as a symbol of hope for the future.

7

MECCA OF THE SEA TURTLE

DR JEANNE A. MORTIMER

'When a green turtle comes ashore she lays roughly a hundred eggs. The eggs are big, round and white, and they seem a great many when you see them all together. The whole race and destiny of the creature are probably balanced at the edge of limbo by the delicate weight of that magic number of eggs. One marvel of the number is how great it is; but another is, how small.'
SO EXCELLENT A FISHE
Archie Carr

Above: A green turtle excavates her egg chamber in the soft sand at the beach-head.
Opposite top: The Malagasey kestrel is a rare sight. It remains to be seen if its invasion of Aldabra will be permanent, or if it suffers a natural extinction as was probably the case with the barn owl.
Opposite: Once famous for its flightless forms, the white-throated rail is the last surviving flightless bird of the Indian Ocean.

151

TODAY, MARINE TURTLES ABOUND IN THE waters of Aldabra. In fact, Aldabra is one of the world's most important breeding and foraging sites for marine turtles. Three species of sea turtles occur regularly at Aldabra. In order of relative abundance these are: the green turtle or *torti-d-mer* (*Chelonia mydas*); the hawksbill turtle or *kare* (*Eretmochelys imbricata*); and the loggerhead turtle (*Caretta caretta*), known as the *torti batar* or *nanmkoyo*. All three species are encountered inside the central lagoon as well as in shallow waters around the perimeter of the atoll. A fourth species, the leatherback turtle or *torti karanbol* (*Kermochelys coriacea*) probably occurs in deep oceanic waters in the vicinity of Aldabra, but has not been recorded at Aldabra itself. (*Karanbol* is the Creole name for the star fruit, whose shape is very similar to the carapace of the leatherback turtle).

The four turtle species can be most easily distinguished from one another by characteristics of their shells and heads. The leatherback is the most distinctive. Its leathery carapace (or upper shell) is black, lacks scales, and has five distinct ridges running longitudinally. Green turtles, hawksbills, and loggerheads all have bony carapaces with three rows of large scales covering the dorsal surface. These include a single row of central scales along the midline flanked on each side by a row of costal scales. The loggerhead turtle typically has five scales in each row. Loggerheads also have very large heads. (They are capable of crushing the giant clam *Tridacna* in their jaws!) Although the scale patterns on the carapaces of both green turtles and hawksbills are the same (five central scales and four scales in each row of costals), the scales of the hawksbill typically overlap like shingles on a roof. Those of the green turtle do not. Another difference between the two species is that the shape of the green turtle head is rounded and blunt. That of the hawksbill turtle is smaller, narrower, and has a pointed 'beak'.

The sex of adult turtles can be determined by looking at the length of the tail and the shape of the claws on the front flippers (external characters cannot be used to tell the sex of juvenile and sub-adult turtles, which all tend to look like females). The tail of the male accommodates the copulatory organ, can measure more than thirty centimetres in length and is muscular and prehensile. The tail of the female is short and rarely extends beyond the hindmost edge of the carapace. The adult male possesses a strong hooked claw on each of his front flippers. In contrast, the claws of the female are relatively short and straight. The male uses these claws much like grappling tools, to secure himself on top of the shell of the female during mating. He hooks his claws onto the anterior edge of the carapace of the female in the shoulder region.

Copulation occurs at sea and may last for several hours. Mating is most commonly observed in nearshore waters adjacent to the nesting beach. At turtle rookeries where the nesting is clearly seasonal, mating occurs early in the season. Because green turtle nesting at Aldabra occurs during every month of the year, mating in this species can also be observed the year round.

Two species of marine turtles nest at Aldabra; the green turtle and the hawksbill.

Although the nesting process is similar for both species, they differ in certain details, such as the time of day when nesting occurs and in the type of gait the animals use to traverse the beach. Aldabran green turtles emerge from the sea at night usually during a medium to high tide (at low tide, they have difficulty crossing the exposed reef flat). The heavy-bodied green turtle laboriously drags itself over the surface of the sand using both front flippers at once. In contrast, Seychelles hawksbills (including those on Aldabra) nest primarily during daylight hours (a preference that sets them apart from the nocturnally nesting hawksbills found in most other parts of the world). The lighter-bodied hawksbill is also able to clamber over rocks and other obstacles with relative ease, alternating her right and left flippers.

After she reaches a satisfactory point above the high tide line, the turtle stops crawling and begins building her 'body pit'. She throws sand backwards using her front flippers until she has created a depression in the sand large enough to accommodate her body. The body pits of green turtles are significantly deeper than those of hawksbills. Using only her rear flippers she then begins constructing her 'egg chamber'. With one flipper she picks up a tea-cup size scoop of sand, drops it on the same side as that flipper and then kicks forward with the opposite flipper. That second flipper then picks up a tea-cup size scoop of sand, drops it to the side, while the first flipper kicks forward (thus kicking out of the way the first scoop

of sand that it dropped). The turtle continues this remarkably delicate process, alternating flippers, never placing the same flipper into the hole twice in succession. Eventually, when the turtle is satisfied with the urn-shaped hole she has constructed, she will begin laying eggs. Green turtles lay about 150 eggs, while hawksbills average about 180 eggs.

The turtle then covers the nest by smoothing sand over the eggs with her rear flippers, camouflages it by throwing large quantities of sand backwards with her front flippers, thus moving the body pit away from the egg clutch, and then returns to the sea. The entire nesting process usually takes less than two hours for hawksbills. For Aldabran green turtles, however, which often dig several nest holes before successfully laying eggs, the process may take considerably longer.

The eggs incubate deep in the sand, warmed only by the sun, for forty-five to fifty-five days. The temperature of incubation determines the sex ratio of the offspring. Warmer temperatures produce relatively more females and cooler temperatures more males. When the baby turtles hatch out of their parchment-shelled eggs, they work instinctively as a group to dig their way to the surface of the sand.

Upon breaking through the surface of the sand, they immediately begin running towards the brightest point on the horizon which, under natural conditions, will take them directly

towards the sea. Once they enter the sea, the hatchlings swim incessantly for several days. They are in the greatest danger from predators in shallow water, so it is important that they reach deep water as quickly as possible.

On virtually every night of the year, green turtles nest at one or more of the forty-seven white, covehead beaches scattered around the perimeter of the atoll. Nesting activity peaks from May to September. Surveys conducted between 1981 and 1985 indicate that during those years an estimated 10,000 to 18,000 green turtle nesting emergences occurred annually on the beaches of Aldabra. All nesting emergences, however, did not culminate in egg-laying. Turtles often have difficulty constructing a suitable egg chamber in the dry, coarse-textured, smooth-grained calcium carbonate sand that characterizes most of the Aldabran green turtle beaches.

As a result, the turtles typically dig several nest holes and emerge on more than one night before successfully laying eggs. Moreover, the average green turtle lays several egg clutches within a given nesting season, returning at approximately two-week intervals to deposit successive clutches. There is evidence that the average green turtle may lay between five and six egg clutches per season. (Some turtles lay only a single egg clutch, while others may lay as many as nine clutches per season). Based on these figures an estimated 800 to 2,100

individual female turtles nested annually at Aldabra during the period of the survey.

Nesting by hawksbill turtles is more restricted, occurring primarily from September to February. At Aldabra, hawksbills typically do not nest on the same beaches as the larger and more abundant green turtles. Rather they nest on the finer-grained calcium carbonate beaches situated in the interior of the lagoon in the vicinity of Main Channel and Passe Houareau. By nesting at these beaches, the hawksbills avoid the possibility of their egg clutches being accidentally excavated by the larger green turtles. They also enjoy the benefit of nesting in finer-grained sand, an easier medium in which to construct a suitable egg chamber, especially for a smaller turtle. The average hawksbill lays about four egg clutches per season. Probably fewer than thirty hawksbills nest annually at Aldabra.

Loggerhead turtles have never been recorded nesting in Seychelles, hence their Creole name *torti batar* or 'bastard turtle'. The Seychellois used to believe that the loggerheads were hybrid turtles which resulted from the mating of a green and a hawksbill turtle. In fact, the loggerheads encountered in Seychelles are most likely members of the breeding populations of Oman, Mozambique, South Africa, and/or Madagascar.

The shallow waters inside the lagoon teem with foraging juvenile and sub-adult green turtles and hawksbills. The hawksbills seem to prefer the open areas at the centre of the

Below: Very few hawksbill turtles breed at Aldabra, their main
Seychelles stronghold being on beaches in the granitic islands.

lagoon and in the passes. Immature green turtles seem most abundant among the tangled
stilt roots of the fringing mangrove forest. Both species can be found in either habitat,
however. The green turtles are herbivores which feed almost exclusively on seagrasses and
algae, while the hawksbills eat primarily sponges and algae.

Small numbers of loggerhead turtles are encountered inside the lagoon. These primarily
carnivorous animals appear to prefer a diet of molluscs and crustaceans.

Adult green turtles are most abundant in the shallow waters adjacent to the outer
perimeter of the atoll. During their breeding season the adult males continue to feed on
seagrasses and algae as they do at other times of the year. Gravid females, however, eat
very little and instead spend much of their time resting.

After leaving the nesting beach the hatchling turtles swim for several days without
stopping. Eventually they will enter driftlines or fronts, areas where two currents meet and
there is a down-welling (or sinking) of water. In these areas, young turtles accumulate in
masses of floating organisms that include other species of animals and plants. Here, they
find food and shelter, and spend the first several years of their lives.

After they have reached the size of a dinner plate, the young turtles move out of the
driftlines and into a shallow foraging habitat. How they locate these foraging grounds is not

known. We do not yet know whether the juvenile and sub-adult green and hawksbill turtles encountered at Aldabra were produced from nesting beaches at Aldabra, or whether Aldabra actually provides foraging grounds for juvenile and sub-adult turtles which come from nesting beaches elsewhere in the Indian Ocean.

Studies are being conducted which involve placing tags on the juvenile and sub-adult turtles encountered at Aldabra. The results of these studies suggest that the immature turtles tend to remain within a relatively restricted area. However, we do not yet know where these same turtles will breed when they eventually reach adulthood. It is hoped that the studies of tagged juvenile and sub-adult turtles at Aldabra will eventually solve this mystery. For at least some populations of turtles, elsewhere in the world, the foraging grounds of the juvenile and sub-adult turtles are located far away from the eventual nesting grounds of those same animals.

Sea turtles take a particularly long time to reach adulthood. There are now excellent data from several places in the world, including Aldabra, which show that green turtles take twenty-five to fifty years to reach maturity and hawksbills take similar periods of time.

To date, three tags placed on nesting females at Aldabra have been returned from Tanzania. This indicates that when the females finish nesting, some, if not all, of the adult turtles leave the vicinity of Aldabra and forage elsewhere. Green turtle females generally do not breed in two successive nesting seasons. Rather, it seems that at the end of a nesting season, a female may spend long intervals of two to eight years (or more), at distant foraging grounds, before returning to breed again.

Today Aldabra is a haven for turtles; but it wasn't always so. During most of the present century, in fact until Aldabra became a nature reserve, hundreds and even thousands of adult green turtles were slaughtered for their meat and calipee (the cartilage linking the carapace and plastron) each year. Only about a kilogramme of calipee can be taken from an adult green turtle. Used to make turtle soup, many thousands of Aldabran green turtles were slaughtered for calipee alone. Large numbers of hawksbill turtles were also killed for their shell. The meat was generally discarded as it is sometimes poisonous. In fact, hawksbill poisoning is fatal in nearly one third of cases, and those who survive often take many months to recover.

The number of female green turtles nesting annually dropped from an estimated 6,000–8,000 at the turn of the century to well below 1,000 during the 1960s and 1970s. Surveys conducted during 1981–1985 indicate an increase in the nesting population over what was recorded during the previous two decades. The fact that nesting activity has remained high since 1985 also gives cause for some optimism for the future of this species on Aldabra.

Since 1968 the Aldabra nesting population has received complete protection. Although more eggs have probably been laid annually since 1968 than before, it is unlikely that hatchlings from those seasons returned to Aldabra as nesting adults as early as the 1980s, for green turtles take much longer than thirteen years to reach sexual maturity. The increase in nesting activity at Aldabra is perhaps better explained by a combination of other factors.

Tagging studies in other parts of the world have shown that female green turtles return repeatedly to the same nesting grounds after intervals of two, three, four, or more years spent at their feeding grounds. After 1968, the slaughter of turtles nesting at Aldabra ceased. Hence, a larger proportion of females nesting in any given year would survive to migrate again to Aldabra in subsequent seasons and to breed again. This probably accounts for much of the observed increase in green turtle nesting activity at Aldabra.

Historical factors may also be responsible, in part, for the observed increase. Between 1945 and 1955 economic factors caused commercial exploitation at Aldabra to lapse temporarily, and between 1948 and 1962, a six-month closed season was established for female turtles at Aldabra. It is probable that relatively fewer females were killed and more eggs laid between 1945 and 1962 than in previous years. The thirty-six years between 1945 and 1981 is probably enough time for turtles hatching in 1945 to attain adulthood and sexual maturity.

Throughout the world, marine turtle populations have been declining as man's greedy exploitation has gathered pace, and in many places the species are endangered. However, Aldabra is one of the few places (Cousin Island in the granitic Seychelles, where hawksbill turtles breed, is another) where there has been an apparent increase in the breeding numbers in recent years. This makes the atoll doubly important since it not only harbours a major population, but it is also a healthy population which appears to be growing back towards its 'natural' state. It is now vital, of course, to ensure that Aldabra's turtle populations remain totally protected so that they can continue to recover and, perhaps, reach the level at which they would have occurred before man's depletion of the stocks. Aldabra's World Heritage Site status underlines the importance of continuing such protection. Perhaps, in years to come, Aldabra's healthy turtle population might be even more valuable as a source for restocking populations which have been over-exploited, or even wiped out, elsewhere.

8

DIVER'S GOLD

WOLFGANG E. GRULKE & DR PHIL C. HEEMSTRA

'As the flow tide began, thousands of fish gathered by the sea gate, waiting to be picked up by the tide and carried into the lagoon…Johnny Channel was in effect a double reef: the opposing walls…were both flower banks of corals…we saw the fish borne away in glittering multitudes on a free ride into the lagoon….The current carried us reeling past lovely corals and around bends….Man and fish in all sorts of distorted positions were frozen in a spatial relationship in the mass of animals streaming through.'
THE LIVING SEA
Captain J.Y. Cousteau

Above: The rich marine life of Aldabra's coral reefs remain pristine and virtually unexplored.
Opposite: Although no longer the exclusive preserve of those able to visit on passing yachts, Aldabra is still one of the world's best-kept secrets.

U

NTIL THE *CALYPSO* EXPEDITION OF JACQUES Cousteau and that of J.L.B. Smith (both in 1954), no specialist studies or collections of the marine fauna of Aldabra had been made. The few records were of scattered species only and gave little appreciation of the overall marine ecology. Since then most expeditions and research work have focused mainly on the terrestrial life and on the marine turtle populations, so the marine ecosystems are still relatively poorly known.

As the world's largest raised coral atoll, Aldabra is made up of a ring of four large and several smaller islands. The thirty-five-kilometre-wide atoll rim encloses a huge tidal lagoon so large that Manhattan could fit comfortably in it. Its shoreline is mainly fossilized coral limestone undercut by the relentless wave action. When you look around from the centre of the lagoon at high tide, you get the impression of being out in the middle of a very calm ocean. At low tide more than eighty per cent of the area of this lagoon may be completely dry. Water covering almost 100 square kilometres has to drain out every low tide and re-enter with every high tide. The islands are separated by deep, narrow channels which form the only way that water can enter or exit the lagoon with the tides. Within these channels lie many of the mushroom-shaped coral outcrops, undercut and shaped by the constant erosion of the tides rushing in and out twice a day.

In this context, Aldabra has several discrete but linked marine environments; the reefs, the lagoon, and the channels. Each of these environments has a character and charm all of its own and the marine inhabitants lead quite different lives.

As with most similar reef environments around the world, the fringing reefs and reef flats, being shallow and well-lit areas, provide the densest profusion and diversity of life imaginable. These are the most complex of living communities. Bathed in strong sunlight for most of the day and washed in constantly warm tropical waters, this is the ideal environment for coral animals to thrive in. The abundance and variety of coral life, in turn, encourages the development of profuse fish and invertebrate communities.

The diversity of fish life on the shallower reefs is amazing. One recent study at Aldabra identified 185 species of fish in just three square kilometres of reef. A variety of butterflyfish, rockcods, triggerfish, hawkfish, parrotfish, scorpionfish, lionfish, angelfish, gobies, fusiliers, lizardfish, rubberlips, and wrasse of every kind are typically seen on every dive. Sea goldies cluster around coral outcrops in large harems.

The sea goldies, *Anthias* spp., are an interesting family, literally the 'goldfish' of the coral reef. They will usually be seen in large active groups around coral heads. Among the many small females there will typically be one larger, dominant, and brightly coloured male. If this dominant male should die, one of the females will immediately begin a transformation and turn into a fully functional spectacular male within just a few days.

Juveniles of the slenderspine grouper, *Gracila albomarginata*, are quite often seen among schools of sea goldies. The juveniles of this species of grouper are spectacularly coloured, violet with broad orange-red stripes on the dorsal and anal fins, and could quite easily be mistaken for boldly coloured male sea goldies. The adult slenderspine groupers are typically

brownish grey with many dark brown bars on the the side of the body. They mostly occur in deeper water.

Fish that are rare in other parts of the Indian Ocean are common in these waters. The emperor angelfish and the regal angelfish, two of the most beautiful examples of the angelfish family, are commonly seen on dives in shallow water.

There are a profusion of gobies, from the shallows at just a few metres deep, right down to the sandy flats at more than forty metres.

Anemones are common, although there is little variety. Most frequently seen are the magnificent or purple base anemone, *Heteractis magnifica* (previously known as *Radianthus ritteri*), rather inappropriately named as it occurs around Aldabra in a variety of colours; crimson, purple, green, and a deep coppery red. The green variety is seen only in the channels leading into the lagoon.

The sand anemone, *Heteractis aurora*, also occurs, inhabiting gravelly sand beds, and retracting completely into the sand at the slightest provocation. The commensal shrimp, *Periclimenes brevicarpalis*, is usually associated with it. The large carpet anemone, *Stichodactyla mertensii* (previously known as *Stoichactis gigas*), is another anemone species seen here, usually in association with the twobar anemonefish, *Amphiprion allardi*. The

Below: Red Gorgonian fan coral with polyps extended to feed on passing nutrients.
Opposite top: The colourful interior of a giant clam contrasts with the camouflaged exterior.
Opposite bottom: Soft tree coral Dendronepthya sp. *supported by spiky calcareous spicules, grows in areas of clean water with a good current flow to supply nutrients.*

nosestripe anemonefish, *Amphiprion akallopisos,* is often observed in association with the magnificent anemone.

Outside the fringing reefs, on the reef slopes between ten and thirty metres in depth, the visibility is generally excellent in the region of twenty to forty metres. The fringing reef drops at an incline of about twenty-five to thirty degrees down to sandy ledges at between twenty to forty metres. Beyond this the profusion of life decreases with the reduced light and the sea bed drops off rapidly into indigo depths. One interesting result of Aldabra's position and structure, as a massive seamount rising from the deep ocean floor, is that the reef is often also visited by pelagic or oceanic species, making it an even more fascinating diving site.

On the reef slopes the coral life is diverse and abundant. Hard corals are, on the whole, more prolific than soft corals there. There are vast colonies of bubble coral *Plerogyra sp.,* in such large groups that they give the impression of being comfortable eiderdowns, swarming with schools of sea goldies. The soft corals develop into absolutely huge colonies.

Plate corals, fragile showpieces, are often the first to show scars from visiting divers, but at Aldabra they are pristine and extremely large. There are colonies of brain coral (*Lobophyllia* sp.), staghorn coral (*Acropora* sp.) and of *Favia* sp. everywhere.

The reef slopes usually end on a sandy ledge or plain between thirty and forty-five metres down. These sandy flats continue to slope down at an average fifteen- to thirty-degree incline to depths in excess of 400 metres. The marine life on these deep sandy ridges varies considerably. Sometimes before the fringing reef finally drops off onto the sandy flats, one finds steep, four- to five-metre underwater cliffs on which huge orange sea fans extend their arms into the nutrient-rich currents. This is typical of the sea bed at forty metres depth just off the West Channels.

At the north-west corner of Aldabra the deep flats are inhabited by a profusion of garden eels that slide gingerly back into their holes when a diver ventures too close. Sharing these sandy flats are a variety of colourful gobies, some with attendant shrimps at the entrance to their holes.

Off the reef near Main Channel there are many different huge orange sponges at about thirty-five metres. Covering the sandy ledge at widely spaced intervals there are also small stunted formations of tubastrea coral (probably *T. micrantha*), one of the few hard corals that can exist at this depth. Here the dark green tubastrea coral looks pitch black and somewhat ominous etched in silhouette against the pure white coral sand. At the north-east end of Aldabra, near Passe Houareau, the same small forests of tubastrea corals dominate the

Below: Yellow-edge moray eel, Gymnothonax flavimarginatus, *feeds on fishes and crustaceans on seaward-facing reefs.*

Opposite: Giant gorgonian fan corals adorn the walls of Aldabra's outer rim.

sandy flats at thirty to forty metres.

Also common at these depths is one of the most beautiful of all corals, *Dendronephthya*. This lovely soft coral is found in the most startling pink, red, white, orange and purple varieties. The delicate polyps extend from thick fleshy stems in which the white spicules are clearly visible. At night its translucent stems are fully expanded to feed and it forms colonies up to one metre high. During the day this soft coral often remains unnoticed as it contracts into modest clumps on the reef substrate.

At night the festive forests of *Dendronephthya sp.* play host to a variety of tiny invertebrate life. Spider-like crabs (most likely a species of *Stenorhynchus*), sporting impossibly long and dainty legs, clamber through this beautiful fairyland. Their coloration and design appear to have specially evolved to cope and blend with this night-time paradise.

There are many hermit crabs. The spectacular *Dardanus megistos* is especially common on the deep sandy ledges and lives in a variety of gastropod shell homes. Not so frequently seen is the unique *Dardanus tinctor*, a hermit crab that purposefully attaches a number of *Calliactis* anemones to its shell, presumably for protection from predators, although there may also be some other mutual benefits from this association.

Main Channel resembles a large river flowing out to sea, except for the fact that at low

Below: Potato cod, Epinephelus tukula, *one of the large resident*
groupers inhabiting the channels to feed on smaller fish
swept along by the strong currents.

*Opposite top: Juvenile oriental sweetlips (*Plectorhinchus gaterinus).
*Opposite bottom: Long-nosed hawkfish (*Oxyirrhites typus)
inhabits gorgonians at depths of more than thirty metres.
*Overleaf: Juvenile hammerhead sharks school (*Sphyrna lewini)
with surgeonfish at the mouth of the channels
awaiting the turn of the tide.

tide it turns around and flows back into the lagoon again! This channel is actually a branching network of channels extending six kilometres into the lagoon at an average depth of about twenty metres. About sixty per cent of the volume of water in the lagoon drains out through Main Channel. At the peak flow at ebb tides, the water has been measured flowing through here at six knots (over ten kilometres per hour), somewhat less than the spectacular estimates of Jacques Cousteau, but still breathtaking when you are in its flow.

This is surely one of Aldabra's unique experiences for the diver. A roller-coaster ride down one of the channels when the tide is flowing in or out, the most incredible drift dive imaginable. In the channels, visibility is often murky due to the strong currents which stir up sea bed and lagoon-floor sediments, but somehow this only serves to add a touch of mystery to the ride.

Coral formations on the edge of the channel are quite limited, and once again the tubastrea hard corals thrive there, presumably because of the high variability of light which makes it difficult for other hard corals to survive because there is not enough consistent light for photosynthesis to take place in their zooxanthellae. Tubastrea, however, has none — so it thrives. Although there are clearly some resident fish (notably large groupers and Napoleon wrasse), most of the population is tidal, literally a 'passing show' that is staged

every six hours or so. Turtles swoop in and out of the diver's field of vision continually. Often there are large schools of unicorn surgeonfish silhouetted against the broken sunlight above. There are also occasional specimens of the large green snail, *Turbo marmoratus,* that were collected almost to extinction during the first half of this century for the manufacture of mother-of-pearl commodities in Europe and the USA. Fortunately, since the invention of man-made substitutes for mother-of-pearl, the frantic hunting has ceased.

A trip past Main Channel along the north coast of Aldabra confirms the uniform geology of the atoll. Apart from a few hundred metres of white coral beaches, the entire coastline of more than eighty kilometres is characterized by low eroded limestone and fossilized coral cliffs that form a mostly impenetrable barrier for man. The sea continually washes up against them, eroding mysterious channels and caves into the rock.

About three kilometres beyond Main Channel, along the north coast, is one of the smaller channels. This is Johnny Channel, a narrow but spectacular island-filled channel that must be one of the most beautiful and fascinating sights on the planet.

The channel is peppered with small mushroom-shaped islets, some on precariously thin stalks. In the mouth of the channel, the water whirls and churns around these islets in its struggle to get into the lagoon. In places small whirlpools are created and instantly diffused. Below the water, stingrays pass over a landscape of coral rubble and a sandy bottom. In the

Below: Yellow rubberlip, Plectorhinchus plagiodesmus, *the largest of
the sweetlips family, is found on coral heads at the mouth of
the channels.*

Opposite: Sea goldies, Anthias squamipinnis *abound in large
active groups around coral heads.*

branching, lesser channels and on much of the lagoon floor adjacent to the channel there is
much dead coral rubble. Among this somewhat bleak terrain are found a few small cowries
and some juvenile triggerfish.

The marine 'night shift' presents an ecology completely different from that seen during
the day. The wrasse, so prolific during the day, hide under the sand at night. Many fish,
notably butterflyfish, adopt quite different colours for their night-time appearance. They are
frequently seen fast asleep within the protective arms of staghorn coral. The spectacular
moorish idol is still easily identified because of its unusual body shape, but its usually
bright, striking coloration is quite matt and dull at night. The yellow and white bands turn
to brown and beige, and its behaviour is positively dozy.

Like many tropical islands, Aldabra is blessed with well developed coral reefs. And, of all
marine fish habitats, coral reefs have the greatest diversity of species. A recent survey of the
fish at the Chagos archipelago in the central Indian Ocean found about 700 species, and
there are probably just as many species at Aldabra. Not only are there hundreds of different
species of fish at Aldabra, but the diversity of shapes, sizes, colours, fin configurations,
mouth structures, food habits, behaviour, and modes of reproduction of coral reef fish are
also amazing. This great diversity of fish is a reflection of the great variety and intricacy of

Below: White-spotted grouper, Epinephelus caeruleopunctatus, *favours coral-rich lagoons and seaward reefs.*

Opposite top: Racoon butterflyfish, Chaetodon lunula, *feed on coral polyps on exposed slopes outside the edge of the reef.*

Opposite bottom: The scissortail sergeant, Abudefduf sexfasciatus, *is found in huge aggregations on the rich coral reefs.*

Overleaf: Sabre squirrelfish are territorial around particular coral heads which become temporary refuges for passing schools of glass-fish.

the habitat. The complexity of the coral reef structure is enhanced by the diversity of plants and invertebrate animals which live on the reef, with the result that there is an abundance of niches into which hundreds of species of fish can be 'fitted'.

Coral reef fish are classified into about 100 families. There is considerable debate among taxonomists about the limits of some fish families, but the vast majority of coral reef species are now grouped into the order Perciformes (the 'typical' perch-like or spiny-rayed fish). Half of all the fish families represented on coral reefs are perciform fish (e.g., butterflyfish, angelfish, damselfish, wrass, parrotfish, surgeonfish, etc.) We still have much to learn about coral reef fish but, thanks to the efforts of ichthyologists in the past few decades, we are beginning to understand the biology and ecological relationships of some species.

Reef fish can be divided into four main groups based on their types of feeding: herbivores, detritivores, carnivores, and omnivores. Because of the high growth rates of their seaweeds, coral reefs are among the most productive habitats on earth, and, as one would expect, there is a huge army of grazing fish that consumes this food resource. Most of the plants consumed are in the form of algal tufts (species less than ten millimetres in height), and mats of filamentous algae. The major herbivorous reef fish are the surgeonfish (Acanthuridae), parrotfish (Scaridae), and the damselfish (Pomacentridae). Other reef fish

that feed on plants are the rabbitfish (Siganidae), chubs (Kyphosidae), some angelfish (Pomacanthidae), some butterflyfish (Chaetodontidae), some blennies (Blennidae) and a few of the gobies (Gobiidae).

Detritus is the fine particulate matter that settles on the reef. The organic component comprises microscopic bits of algae, fish faeces and the invertebrate animals that live on the reef, dead plankton, and other dead microscopic forms of life such as benthic diatoms, dinoflagellates and bacteria. The inorganic component of detritus comprises microscopic bits of pulverized corals or coralline algae, fine sand and sediment grains, shells from planktonic protozoans, etc. The organic component of detritus can be very nutritious, and some fish feed primarily on detritus. Many herbivores (e.g., Centrypyge angelfish) also ingest greater or lesser amounts of detritus, and some detritivores (e.g., the striped bristletooth *Ctenochaetus striatus*) also eat some forms of live algae.

Some fish are carnivorous. Some are specialized to feed on plankton, and the fusiliers (Caesionidae) are probably the most conspicuous of the plankton eaters on the coral reef. Most reef fish larvae and small juveniles feed on plankton, but adult plankton eaters, such as the fusiliers, with their streamlined bodies and forked caudal fins, protrusile mouths, and numerous long gill-rakers, are specially adapted for feeding on the small zooplankton in the

Below: The longfin bannerfish, Heniochus acuminatus, *is a species of deep lagoons and seaward reefs which feeds primarily on zooplankton.*

Below: The longfin bannerfish, Heniochus acuminatus, *is a species of deep lagoons and seaward reefs which feeds primarily on zooplankton.*

currents passing over the reef. Almost every fish family on the reef has some species that have specialized in plankton feeding: for example, in the Serranidae, *Anthias*, *Mirolabrichthys* and *Nemanthias*. Also like the fusiliers, these plankton eaters are active by day; at dusk, they retire to the reef and can be found resting under ledges and hiding among the coral during the hours of darkness. At night, a new cast of plankton-eating fish moves onto the stage: e.g. soldierfish (*Myripristis* spp.), bigeyes (*Priacanthus* spp.) and cardinalfish (*Apogon* spp.). The zooplankton food of these nocturnal hunters is larger (mostly more than two millimetres) than the prey of the diurnal feeders, simply because the smaller zooplankton is more difficult to see at night.

The prey of the other reef fish carnivores can be grouped into four categories: sessile invertebrates (such as corals and sponges), small cryptic invertebrates (such as crustaceans, brittlestars and polychaetes), macroinvertebrates (such as crustaceans, molluscs and sea urchins), and fishes. Juvenile fish and adults with small mouths (e.g. butterflyfish and most wrasses) feed primarily on small crustaceans and other cryptic invertebrates. Some parrotfish and many butterflyfish feed on living coral. The parrotfish, with their beak-like fused teeth and powerful jaws, simply bite off chunks of coral which are then crushed by their mill-like pharyngeal teeth and swallowed. The coral tissue and symbiotic algae are digested as the crushed coral moves through the intestine, and the fine coral residue is passed out of the anus as a cloud of white sediment, a scene often observed by scuba divers. Butterflyfish, with their small delicate mouths, bite off the coral's fleshy little polyps. The larger reef predators take a variety of crustaceans, molluscs, echinoderms, and fishes as their prey. Some of them, such as the barracuda and *Caranx* spp. are primarily fish eaters. However, most emperor fish (Lethrinidae) feed at night on hard-shelled invertebrates such as crustaceans, bivalves, gastropods and sea urchins.

A very specialized category of carnivores includes the cleaner fish, which feed on the ectoparasites that they remove from the skin of other fish. The cleaner wrasse, *Labroides dimidiatus*, establishes 'cleaning stations' where other fish congregate to be cleaned of their parasites. Juveniles of some fish (e.g., wrasse of the genus *Bodianus*) may feed as cleaners, but later in life they acquire other food habits. Off Aldabra's west coast there are so many cleaner stations in some areas that they create serious congestion as fish jostle for attention. The juvenile wrasse, *Bodianus axillaris*, are also seen cleaning a variety of large rockcods.

The ecology of reef fish is an enormous study. Each species has a unique solution to the problems of finding food, avoiding predators and reproduction. Watching fish and other reef animals go about their business, we get the impression of a complex and busy community. Space (rather than food) seems to be the limiting factor on the number of fish that the reef can support. This impression is reinforced on a night dive, when we see many fish and invertebrates that were not apparent during the day, but are now out and about feeding or foraging. We still have much to learn of the interactions of the animals and plants of the beautiful, complex, and dynamic community that is a coral reef, and Aldabra is a unique laboratory for the amateur and professional marine naturalist alike.

With such a profusion and abundance of life everywhere, what does a natural paradise like Aldabra not have? Well, there are relatively few echinoderms, that is, starfish, sea cucumbers and sea urchins. Shell life, too, is rather limited in terms of variety. There are few moray eels, only two species of anemonefish, few flatworms and nudibranchs, and no Spanish dancers. However, the reasons for this are unknown and must be investigated. In the meantime, the coral reef of Aldabra is a veritable plethora of life and beauty.

Anyone who sees Aldabra atoll above or below sea level, must feel greatly privileged to have witnessed this unique island. Let us hope that future generations will also have the opportunity to experience the privilege of visiting Aldabra.

PHOTOGRAPHERS

Len Mole joined the Royal Society as Expeditions Officer in 1968 with the prime task of constructing the Aldabra research station, followed by the responsibility for management, servicing and staffing up to 1980, when responsibility was transferred to the Seychelles Islands Foundation. He has continued to assist the foundation in an honorary capacity mainly in the UK. He continues to work for the Royal Society, based in London.

Dr Phil Plummer is an Australian geoscientist, currently contracted to the Seychelles National Oil Company Ltd. His speciality is interpretation of geological concepts from geophysical data and he has actively fulfilled this function in the Netherlands, the Middle East, East and West Africa as well as Australia and New Zealand prior to arriving in Seychelles in 1990. He gained his PhD degree from Adelaide University, South Australia. He edited the proceedings of an international petroleum seminar in Seychelles, and published a score of technical papers in scientific journals, and several photo-travelogues in magazines.

Mohamed Amin is a photographer and cameraman who has filmed major events in Africa, Asia and the Middle East since the 1950s. Awarded an MBE in 1992, his many international awards include Britain's 'Valiant for Truth' Award, the British Academy of Film and Television Arts Award, the Royal Television Society's Judge's Award, and the Guild of Television 'Camermen's Cameraman' Award. A Fellow of the Royal Geographical Society, he holds one of Pakistan's highest civil honours, the Tamgha-i-Imtiaz. He has photographically illustrated over forty books, including several on Seychelles.

Duncan Willetts is one of Africa's and Europe's major creative photographers. A regular contributor to *Time-Life*, *Newsweek* and other major magazines and newspapers around the world, he has contributed photographically to many books with Mohamed Amin, including the *Spectrum Guides* to Kenya, Pakistan, Zimbabwe, Tanzania, Maldives, Namibia, Jordan, African Wildlife Safaris, and Seychelles, together with *Journey Through Pakistan, Journey Through Kenya, Journey Through Nepal, Journey Through Maldives, Journey Through Tanzania, Journey Through Zimbabwe*, and *Journey Through Seychelles*.

Judith Skerrett is a writer and historian who has lived in Seychelles since 1980. She is co-author of *Beautiful Plants of Seychelles, Beauty of Seychelles, Journey Through Seychelles, Insight Pocket Guide to Seychelles*, and *Spectrum Guide to Seychelles*. She is editor of RSNC's *Aride Island Newsletter* and has contributed articles on Seychelles to *The Guardian, Irish Times, Woman's Weekly, Silhouette*, and many others.

Background: A lone mangrove tree stands sentinel in the lagoon at low tide.

All pictures taken by **Mohamed Amin** and **Duncan Willetts** except the following:

Adrian Skerrett: 82 (top), 85 (left), 93, 96, 98, 121, 129, 137 (top left), 138 (bottom left, top right, centre right), 143 (bottom left, top right), 150.
Lindsay Chong-Seng: 74, 107, 109.
Ron Gerlach: 82 (bottom left), 95, 106.
Bruce Schoeberl: 137 (centre right), 145 (right).
Ruth Prendergast: 154.
David Rowat: 156.

BIBLIOGRAPHY

Amoco Seychelles Petroleum Co., 1983 Interpretation and operations report of a high sensitivity aeromagnetic survey over the Seychelles Bank. *Hunting Geological Geophysical Ltd.* Survey 210199 (Unpubl.).

Arnold, E.N., 1985 Fossil Reptiles from Aldabra Atoll, Indian Ocean. *Bulletin of the British Museum (Natural History)* **29**(3): 85–116.

Attenborough, D., 1984 *The Living Planet.* Collins/BBC, London.

Baker, B.H., 1963 Geology and mineral resources of the Seychelles Archipelago. *Geological Survey of Kenya* Mem. 3.

Beamish, T., 1970 *Aldabra Alone.* George Allen & Unwin, London.

Benson, C.W., 1967 The birds of Aldabra and their status. *Atoll Research Bulletin* **118**: 63–111.

Benson, C.W. & Penny, M.J., 1971 The land birds of Aldabra. *Philosophical Transactions of the Royal Society of London* B260: 417–527.

Bradley, J.T., 1936 *History of the Seychelles Islands.* Clarion Press, Seychelles.

Bradley, J.T., 1940 The History of Seychelles Parts 1 & 2. Seychelles.

Braithwaite, C.J.R., Taylor, J.D. & Kennedy, W.J., 1973 The evolution of an atoll: The depositional and erosional history of Aldabra. *Philosophical Transactions of the Royal Society of London* B266: 307–40.

Branch, B., 1988 *Field guide to the snakes and other reptiles of Southern Africa.* Struik Publishers.

Bruggen, A.C. van, 1975 Streptaxidae (Mollusca, Gastropoda: Pulmonata) from Aldabra Island, Western Indian Ocean. *Bulletin of the British Museum of Natural History (Zool.)* **28**(5): 157–75.

Bulpin, T.V., 1969 *Islands in a Forgotten Sea.* Books of Africa

Carr, A., 1967 *So Excellent a Fishe.* Charles Scribner's Sons, New York.

Cherbonnier, G., 1964 *Aldabra L'Ile aux Tortues Géantes.* Gedalge, Paris.

Cousteau, J.Y., 1959 *Aldabra Sanctuaire de Corail.* Ima, Paris.

Cousteau, J.Y., 1963 *The Living Sea.* Harper & Row, New York.

Darwin, C., 1839 *Journal of Researches into the Geology and Natural History of the Various Countries visited by HMS "Beagle", under the Command of Captain Fitzroy, RN, from 1832 to 1836.* Henry Colburn, London.

Diamond, A.W., 1971 *The ecology of the sea birds of Aldabra. Philosophical Transactions of the Royal Society of London* B260: 561–71.

Diamond, A.W., 1974 The Red-footed Booby on Aldabra atoll, Indian Ocean. *Ardea* **62**: 196–218.

Diamond, A.W., 1975 Biology and behaviour of Frigatebirds *Fregata spp* on Aldabra atoll. Ibis 117: 302–23.

Diamond, A.W., 1975 The biology of tropicbirds of Aldabra atoll, Indian Ocean. *Auk* 92: 16–39.

Diamond, A.W., 1979 Dynamic ecology of Aldabran seabird communities. *Philosophical Transactions of the Royal Society of London* B286: 231–40.

Falck, K., 1965 Norwegian Trade, Shipping & Colonisation in Madagascar 1865–1888. in *Norwegian Yearbook of Maritime History 1965*, Bergens Sjofartsmuseum, Bergen.

Fauvel, A.A., 1909 Unpublished Documents on the History of the Seychelles Anterior to 1810. Government Printer, Seychelles.

Feare, C.J., 1978 The decline of Booby (Sulidae) populations in the western Indian Ocean. *Biological Conservation* (14): 295–305.

Ferrara, F. & Taiti, S., 1985 The Terrestrial Isopods (Crustacea) of Aldabra. *Zoological Journal of the Linnaean Society* **85**: 291–315.

Frazier, J., 1971 Observations on sea turtles at Aldabra Atoll. Philosophical Transactions of the Royal Society of London, series B **260**:373-410.

Frazier, J., 1976 Report on sea turtles in the Seychelles area. Journal of the Marine Biological Association of India **18**(2):1-63.

Friedmann, F., 1986 Avatars Insulaires. *L'Univers du Vivant* 15: 75–81.

Friedmann, F., 1986 *Flowers and Trees of Seychelles.* Editions Delroisse for Department of Finance, Seychelles.

Fosberg, F.R. & Renvoize, S.A., 1980 The Flora of Aldabra and Neighbouring Islands. *Kew Bulletin Additional Series VII*, HMSO, London.

Frith, C.B., 1976 A twelve month field study of the Aldabran Fody *Foudia eminentissima aldabrana. Ibis* **118**: 2 155–78.

Frith, C.B., 1977 Life history notes on some Aldabran land birds. *Atoll Res. Bull.* **201**: 1-17.

Fryer, J.C.F., 1911. The structure and formation of Aldabra and neighbouring islands, with notes on their flora and fauna. *Transactions of the Linnaean Society of London 2 (Zool)*14: 397–411.

Gaillard, G., Bernier, P., & Gruet, Y., 1992 Le Lagon d'Aldabra (Seychelles), Un modèle pour le Paleomilieu de Cerin (Kimmeridgien Superieur, France). *Geobios, Supplement 1 Memoire Special* **16**: 22.

Gardener, A.S., 1985 An identification key to the geckos of the Seychelles, with brief notes on their distribution and habits. *Herpetological Journal* Vol 1: 17-19.

Gardener, A.S., 1988 Day geckos of the genus *Phelsuma* in the outer Seychelles. *Biological Society of Washington Bulletin* 8: 101–7.

Gerlach, J., 1987 *The Land Snails of Seychelles — A Field Guide.* Privately published.

Gerlach, J. & Canning, K.L., 1994 On the crocodiles of the western Indian Ocean. *Phelsuma* 2.

Gibson, T.S.H., 1979 Green turtle (*Chelonia mydas* (L.)) nesting activity at Aldabra Atoll. *Philosophical Transactions of the Royal Society of London, series B* **286**: 255-263

Grubb, P., 1971 Ecology of terrestrial decapod crustaceans on Aldabra. *Philosophical Transactions of the Royal Society of London* B260: 411–16.

Hill, J.E., 1971 The bats of Aldabra Atoll, western Indian Ocean. *Philosophical Transactions of the Royal Society of London* B260: 573–6.

Hirth, H. and A. Carr., 1970 The green turtle in the Gulf of Aden and the Seychelles Islands. *Verhandelingen der Koninklijke Nederlandse Akademie van Wetenschappen. Afd. Natuurkunde* 58(5): 1-44.

Hornell, J., 1927 *The turtle fisheries of the Seychelles Islands.* H.M. Stationery Office, London. 55pp.

Hoyt, E.P. Jnr., 1946 *The Germans Who Never Lost.* Leslie Frewin, London.

Legrand, H., 1965 Lepidopteres des iles Seychelles et d'Aldabra. *Memoires of the Museum of Natural History,*

Paris Series A (Zool) **27**: 210.

LeGeyt, Capt. P.S., 1961 *Makarios in Exile*. Anagennisis Press, Nicosaia.

Linfield, M.C.J., Raubenheimer, D., Hambler, C., & Speight, M.R., 1993 Leaf miners on Ochna ciliata (*Ochnaceae*) growing on Aldabra Atoll: patterns of herbivory in relation to goat browsing and exposure to the sun. *Ecological Entomology* **18**: 332–8.

Lionnet, G., 1972 *The Seychelles*. David & Charles, Newton Abbot.

Lowe, K.W & Richards, G.C., 1991 Morphological variation in the Sacred Ibis *Threskiornis aethiopicus superspecies* complex. *Emu* Vol **91**: 41–5.

McAteer, W., 1991 *Rivals in Eden*. The Book Guild, Sussex.

McCloy. B., 1984 The Aldabra Post Office. *Stamp Collecting* **148**: 25(3668).

Matthiessen, P., 1971 *Blue Meridian*. Random House, N.Y.

Moresby, Capt. F., 1842 *On The Seychelles Islands*. Nautical Magazine & Naval Chronicle Enlarged Series No 9 Vol for 1842: 585. (*Seychelles National Archives Document F/2.421*).

Mortimer, J.A., 1984 *Marine Turtles in the Republic of the Seychelles*. IUCN/WWF.

Mortimer, J.A., 1985 Recovery of green turtles on Aldabra. *Oryx* **19**(3): 146-150.

Mortimer, J.A., 1988 Green turtle nesting at Aldabra Atoll — population estimates and trends. *Bulletin of the Biological Society of Washington* 8:116-128.

Mortimer, J.A. & R. Bresson, 1994 The hawksbill nesting population at Cousin Island, Republic of Seychelles: 1971-1992. p. 115-117. In: B.A. Schroeder and B.E. Witherington (compilers), *Proceedings of the Thirteenth Annual Symposium on Sea Turtle Biology and Conservation. NOAA Technical Memorandum NMFS-SEFSC-341*.

Nicoll, M.J., 1908 *Three Voyages of a Naturalist*. Witherby & Co., London.

Ommanney, F.D., 1952 *The Shoals of Capricorn*. Harcourt, Brace & Co., New York.

Penny, M.J. & Diamond, A.W., 1971 The White-throated Rail *Dryolimnas cuvieri* on Aldabra. *Philosophical Transactions of the Royal Society of London* B260: 529–548.

Prys-Jones, R.P., 1979 The ecology and conservation of the Aldabra Brush Warbler *Nesillas aldabranus*. *Philosophical Transactions of the Royal Society of London* B286: 211–24.

Prys-Jones, R.P., 1980 Breeding periodicity, nesting success and nest site selection among Red-tailed Tropicbirds *Phaethon rubricauda* and White-tailed Tropicbirds *P. lepturus* on Aldabra atoll. *Ibis* **122**: 76–81.

Reville, B.J., 1983 Numbers of nesting Frigatebirds, *Fregata minor* and *F. ariel*, on Aldabra atoll nature reserve, Seychelles. *Biol. Cons.* **27**: 59–76.

Reville, B.J., 1988 Effects of spacing and synchrony on breeding success in the Great Frigatebird (*Fregata minor*). *Auk* **105**: 252–9.

Reville, B.J., 1991 Nest spacing and breeding success in the Lesser Frigatebird (*Fregata ariel*). *The Condor* **93**: 555–62.

Ridgway, R., 1895 On birds collected by W.L. Abbott in the Seychelles, Amirantes, Gloriosa, Assumption, Aldabra and adjacent islands with notes on habits, etc., by the collector. *Proceedings of the United States National Museum*, Vol XVIII, No.1079: 509–46.

Rivers, F., 1878 Report of a Visit to Aldabra and Other Islands of the Cosmoledo Group on Board the "Flower of Jarrow". (*Seychelles National Archives Document D/12./93*)

Roberts, P., 1987 Is the Aldabra Brush Warbler extinct? *Oryx* **21**: 209–10.

Robertson, M., 1991 Husbandry and moulting behaviour of the Robber or Coconut crab *Birgus latro*. *International Zoological Yearbook* **30**: 60–67.

Robertson, S.A., 1989 *Flowering Plants of Seychelles*. Royal Botanic Gardens Kew.

Seaton, A.J. et al., 1991 A Focus on Aldabra. *Conserving the Environment* No. 3, Ministry of Education, Seychelles.

Seychelles National Archives, *Correspondence Relating to the Aldabra Group 1829–1943*. (Seychelles National Archives Document c/55/73).

Seychelles National Archives, *Seychelles Historical Records* Vol XIV.

Seychelles National Archives, (Seychelles National Archives Document 48B 37)

Skerrett, A., & Skerrett, J., 1990 *Spectrum Guide to Seychelles*. Camerapix Publishers International Nairobi.

Skerrett, A., & Bullock, I., 1992 *A Birdwatchers' Guide to Seychelles*. Prion Perry.

Smith, M. & Heemstra, P., 1986 *Smith's Sea Fishes*. Springer Verlag, South Africa.

Stoddart, D.R., 1967 Geography and Ecology of Aldabra Atoll. *Atoll Res. Bull.* **118**: 11–52.

Stoddart, D.R., Taylor, J.D., Fosberg, F.R., & Farrow, G.E., 1971. Geomorphology of Aldabra Atoll. *Philosophical Transactions of the Royal Society of London* B260: 31-65.

Stoddart, D.R., 1973 Coral reefs: The last two million years. *Geography* **58**(4): 313–23.

Stoddart, D.R., 1976 *The green turtle trade of Aldabra and Seychelles*. [mimeographed, 25pp]

Stoddart, D.R. et al., 1979 *The Terrestrial Ecology of Aldabra*. The Royal Society, London.

Stoddart, D.R., 1983 Aldabra Atoll: A Stunning Success Story for Conservation. *Nature & Resources* **19**(1): 20–28.

Stoddart, D.R. (ed.), 1984 *Biogeography and Ecology of the Seychelles Islands*. Dr. W. Junk Publishers, The Hague.

Taylor, J.D., Braithwaite, C.J.R, Peake, J.F., & Arnold, E.N., 1979 Terrestrial faunas and habitats of Aldabra during the Pleistocene. *Philosophical Transactions of the Royal Society of London* B260: 47–66.

Thomson, J. & Walton, A., 1972. Redetermination of chronology of Aldabra Atoll by 230Th/234U dating. *Nature* **240** (5377): 145–6.

Trudgill, S.T., 1972. Quantification of limestone erosion in intertidal, subaerial and subsoil environments, with special reference to Aldabra Atoll, Indian Ocean. *Transactions of the Cave Research Group of Great Britain* **14**(2): 176–9.

Woodell, R., 1976 Notes on the Aldabran Coucal *Centropus toulou insularis*. *Ibis* **118**: 263–8.

Wright, C.A., 1971 Bulinus on Aldabra and the subfamily Bulininae in the Indian Ocean. *Philosophical Transactions of the Royal Society of London* B260: 299–314.

Overleaf: A giant tortoise makes its way towards shelter for the night through the cool of dusk.
Page 192: A golden sunset marks the end of another day on Aldabra.